HIGH UINTA TRAILS

In God's wilderness lies the hope of the world — the great, fresh, unblighted, unredeemed wilderness. The galling harness of civilization drops off, and the wounds heal ere we are aware.

— *John Muir*

HIGH UINTA TRAILS

A Hiking and Backpacking Guide
to the High Uintas Wilderness and Surrounding Areas

By Mel Davis
Updated By John Veranth

CREDITS

FRONT COVER/   Ostler Peak, Dave Wallace
                       Marmot, John Veranth

BACK COVER/   Porcupine Pass, Dave Wallace
                       Deer Lake, John Veranth

SKETCHES/   Lois Kyle Snyder
                       Margaret Pettis

TRAIL MAPS/   Mel Davis

Wasatch Publishers
4460 Ashford Drive
Salt Lake City, Utah 84124

ISBN 0-915272-37-7

4

KINGS PEAK

Contents

Acknowledgement (1974 Edition)

The editor wishes to express his appreciation to the following sources for their splendid cooperation:

Jerry Horton, Supervisor's Office, Wasatch National Forest
Kent Taylor, Supervisor's Office, Ashley National Forest
Bill Sims, Roosevelt Ranger District, Ashley National Forest
Al Ashton, Duchesne Ranger District, Ashley National Forest
Eldon Wilkins, Duchesne Ranger District, Ashley National Forest
Earl O'Driscoll, Evanston Ranger District, Wasatch National Forest
Steve Scott, Kamas Ranger District, Wasatch National Forest
Sam Allan, Wasatch Mountain Club
Utah Division of Wildlife Resources

Acknowledgement (1993 Revision)

The information for this update came from many sources. The co-author and editor wish to first thank Mel Davis for publishing the original guidebook that accompanied us on many trips to the Uintas. Also thanks to the members of the Wasatch Mountain Club who introduced us to many of the trails in Utah.

Field checkers included Duke Moscon, Reni Stott, and Jon Eagar. The Utah Wilderness Association staff: George Nickas, Gary MacFarlane, and Dick Carter, contributed their extensive knowledge of both the backcountry and of the management issues.

Photographs were provided by Dave Wallace, Thad Eagar, and by Tom Pettingill and Jerry Weichman of the Utah Division of Wildlife Resources. Sketches from the original edition are by Lois Kyle Snyder and new sketches were furnished by Margaret Pettis.

Typing the 1974 draft into a word processor was done by Alison Hottes. Editing was done by Martha Morrison Veranth.

Detailed information regarding trailhead and backcountry conditions was again provided by Forest Service staff including:

Wasatch National Forest
Kamas Ranger District: Melissa Blackwell, Mead Hargas, Black George
Evanston Ranger District: Steve Ryberg, Earl O'Driscoll
Mountain View Ranger District: Rick Schuler

Ashley National Forest
Duchesne Ranger District: Sue White, Chris Bollinger
Roosevelt Ranger District: Bill Sims, Gayne Sears
Vernal Ranger District: Mike Bergfeld
Flaming Gorge Ranger District: John Neeling

A Word of Caution

This guide was compiled from many sources and provides information that was believed to be reliable at the time of publication. The reader is expected to have the necessary skill to deal with natural hazards including route conditions, stream crossings, wildlife, and weather.

Individuals must evaluate their own physical condition, outdoor experience, food, footwear, and equipment before attempting any particular trail or route.

Notes on Information in This Book

The USGS topographic maps listed for each trailhead include the maps covering the main trail and major destinations in that drainage. Maps that are optional maps because the trail crosses only a corner or edge of the sheet are marked " * ."

Tables of mileages and elevation changes were determined from topographic maps. The listed elevation change contains both uphill sections when the trail crosses a major pass then drops to a stream and climbs again. Minor up and down sections were not calculated so elevations are rounded to 100 feet.

Fishing information was based on Utah Division of Wildlife Resources sources. Changes in fish stocking programs will alter species populations.

Picture Lake in East Basin of Lake Fork / Mel Davis Photo.
(Cover of original edition)

Preface

This guidebook is a completely rewritten edition of High Uinta Trails. The first High Uintas edition of this guidebook, written by Mel Davis in 1974, introduced thousands of hikers, backpackers, horse riders, and anglers to the trails, lakes and mountains of the Uintas. The mountains and lakes are unchanging on the scale of human lifetimes but political designations, roads, and even the backcountry trails do change so guidebooks need periodic updating.

Trailheads have been reconstructed and improved, access roads have been upgraded or paved, and some old landmarks have disappeared. Backcountry trail crews have reconstructed some routes while the natural processes of erosion, mud slides, and growing vegetation continue to erase others.

In 1984 Congress designated the High Uintas Wilderness which included virtually all of the old High Uintas Primitive Area plus additional wild and natural lands around the edges. Wilderness designation has changed Forest Service management. Human intrusions including semi-permanent ranger camps and even the large, highly-visible signs have been phased out from the Wilderness. These have been replaced by ranger patrols and smaller unpainted wood signs at major trail junctions.

There is additional emphasis in this revision on off-trail routes and on summit climbs. Some worthwhile trails outside the Wilderness have been added to call attention to the natural values found in nearby areas that are not officially protected. Wilderness ethics and backpacking techniques have been updated to reflect the ever-increasing backcountry use and to express the latest thinking on minimizing human impact.

CAIRN

Top: Beaver dam on a wild and healthy stream. / John Veranth Photo
Bottom: Looking north from Ostler Pass / Dave Wallace Photo

THE HIGH UINTAS -
An Ecosystem Vision

By Dick Carter

The High Uintas are a massive, forested remnant defined by water and true alpine basins; truly a unique place in Utah. Walter Cottam, one of Utah's preeminent botanists, noted in 1930 that "the Uinta Mountains represents Utah's only claim to a typical Northern Rocky Mountain Flora." In fact, the area above timberline in a true alpine flora on the Uintas alone exceeds all the other alpine areas within the Intermountain West. Along with the most extensive alpine terrain, the Uintas host the most extensive continuous forest in the Intermountain West.

The Uintas are the headwaters where Utah's major rivers burst into life. Hundreds of glacially carved lakes dot small and large alpine basins. The Uintas were extensively glaciated and while glaciers no longer find refuge in these mountains the land is still shaped by the harshest weather one can imagine.

The North Slope is a gentle, almost plateau-like region of dense lodgepole pine forests surrounding meandering open parklands and high mountain meadows. River bottoms are wide and filled with willows and potholes and beaver ponds — an idyllic setting for moose! A hike up any of the major drainages eventually leads to the rugged crest of the range. From the ridge tops one can see the heart of the Uintas and the massiveness of the area is displayed in its full majesty.

Off in the distance are deep glacial canyons lost in the jumble of mile after mile of spruce and fir forests gently tumbling into the lodgepole pine. On the South Slope long river drainages lead down from some of the most spectacular alpine basins in the United States. The Yellowstone River glides over 20 miles from its headwaters below Kings Peak to the trailhead, while the Uinta River slices an 80-foot vertical gorge in the floor of the mountain's largest glacial canyon.

This diversity and size allow the Uintas to harbor the most unique and sensitive fauna in the Intermountain West. Canada lynx, black bear, cougar, great grey owl, boreal owl, golden eagles, goshawks, osprey, pine marten, ptarmigan, river otter, Rocky Mountain bighorn sheep, moose and elk inhabit the Uintas. Grizzly bear, timber wolf, bison and wolverine once called the Uintas a secure home. Although fragmented by timber harvesting, grazing, dam building, predator control, and oil and gas development as well as by state wildlife management activities focusing primarily on game management, the Uintas have shown a tough resiliency. They are a biologically important and largely intact mountain sanctuary. Yet only upper reaches of the mountains are protected. Wilderness lands are protected from the ravages of timber harvesting, mining, and oil drilling, but that alone is not enough. Many areas show extensive damage, particularly around lakes and along trails. Fire rings, camp structures, hacked trees, bare soil, and overgrazed meadows impair the integrity of wild country. Management too has taken a toll on naturalness. The lack of ecologically-based wildlife management has created unnatural populations and demographics. Native cutthroat trout have been replaced by non-native, more productive game fishes. Wildlife management has favored game production over conservation of biological diversity and non-consumptive viewing.

Although the range has been partially protected as a National Forest for nearly a century and as a Primitive Area since 1931, its roadless nature has been steadily eroded by logging and energy development.

Start hiking at almost any trailhead. Wind gradually upward through deep old-growth forest of lodgepole pine, spruce and fir, past willow-filled meadows with browsing moose, and along icy-clear streams fresh from their snowfall beginnings. After a while, sometimes several hours of tranquil hiking, you will see the sign — "High Uintas Wilderness" — denoting the artificial boundary that separates the protected Wilderness from the unprotected.

The Utah Wilderness Act of 1984 omitted critical lands. About 30,000 acres of roadless land along the North Slope from the Bear River to Blacks Fork were not considered. On the eastern end the Whiterocks, Ashley Creek, and Sheep Creek country, collectively known as "The Bollies," contains another 100,000 acres of unprotected wild terrain. The task of protecting the remaining wild lands, unroaded and roaded, is far from complete.

The range also needs protection for the lower forest basins and for entire drainages. It needs a vision that a salamander is every bit as important as a trout. It needs recognition of the forest primeval as the critical value. It needs protection not only for wilderness or potential wilderness but for the lands that have already been abused. We cannot have a healthy wilderness surrounded by reckless development. Sensitive land management must complement wilderness and wilderness must allow for sustainable land management emphasizing a healthy ecosystem outside of wilderness.

Timber harvesting plans need to be revised to reflect biodiversity-sustaining harvest levels. Harvesting must concentrate on managing the already impacted areas and new cutting in roadless areas must stop. Inactive oil project sites need to be reclaimed and restored before new areas are committed to development.

Solutions are needed to conflicts between domestic sheep and recreation, wildlife (especially bighorn sheep), and watersheds. Significant ungrazed habitats must be provided to allow native plants and animals to populate a functioning ecosystem shaped by evolution and not manipulated for human gain. A recovery plan for pine marten, lynx, black bear, wolverine, and native cutthroat trout will illuminate the promise of a wild Uintas.

Saving Utah's wildest ecosystem is a long-term commitment. Thousands visit the Uintas each year, but sadly, too few take an active role in their defense. Contact the Forest Service and express your support for biodiversity and protection of the Uintas ecosystem. Support the citizen conservation groups (addresses in the Appendix) and get involved.

Dick Carter is Coordinator of the Utah Wilderness Association and has spent many years advocating sound land and wildlife management.

On the trail from Grandaddy Lake back to Grandview Trailhead
John Veranth Photo

HIKING THE UINTAS -
An Introduction

The Uinta Mountains are awesome. The outstanding mountain scenery, wildlife, and wilderness qualities create a memorable experience for all who take the time to explore.

The range is named after the "Uintats" Indians who were mountain dwellers and a branch of the Ute Tribe. The first Europeans to discover the Uinta trails were the fur trappers. They were followed by the government explorers, Powell, King, and Hayden, leading the post-Civil War Territorial Surveys that documented the area. The major drainages have been exploited for timber and grazing but the natural values were recognized early.

The High Uintas Primitive Area was established in 1931. On September 28, 1984 Congress designated the 456,700 "High Uintas Wilderness" as part of a state-wide Forest Service Wilderness Bill. The new Wilderness included most of the Primitive Area plus some major additions to the east between Kings Peak and Island Lake. There were a few other additions around the edges and some deletions for reservoirs on the South Slope. Overall it was a big gain for protection.

The Uinta Mountains are the crest of a broad uplift 150 miles long and 35 miles wide. Elevations vary from about 8,000 feet in the lower canyons to 13,528 feet at the highest point in Utah, the summit of Kings Peak. The Uintas are often called "the most prominent east-west range in the United States." In fact, there are other east-west ranges; the Brooks Range in Alaska is longer, and the Santa Monica Mountains in Los Angeles are certainly more conspicuous.

The backbone of the range is a rugged chain of peaks and precipitous slopes flanked by flat-topped mountains that are remnants of the uplifted surface. Canyons, gorges, basins, and talus slopes of spectacular beauty have been created as the streams and glaciers carved into the broad plateaus. The core of the range consists of multi-colored quartzites and shales of Precambrian age. The upturned edges of younger sedimentary rock layers are found around the perimeter of the range. These formations dip deep under the fossil-fuel-rich Uinta Basin and reappear to form the spectacular Book Cliffs and Canyon Country of southern Utah.

Ridges running north and south from the main crest divide the area into long, branching, independent basins. The dense forest, gravel soils and rocky moraines on the floor of these basins are a spectacular contrast with the abrupt ridges which tower several thousand feet above. There are over 1000 natural lakes and many more small ponds and potholes scattered throughout the Wilderness. Utah Wildlife Resources reports that more than 650 lakes currently contain game fish.

The Wilderness is for all types of non-mechanized recreation: day hiking, backpacking, horse riding, mountain climbing, nature study, taking pictures, fishing, or just enjoying beauty and quiet solitude. It is a huge, wild, picturesque region, rich in scenic, geological and biological interest.

One-day trips from any trailhead will provide a sampling of enjoyable wilderness experiences. Trips of three days or more present the hiker with unexcelled scenery. Vistas change in short distances as do the geology and ecology. The heaviest usage of the area is within a day's hike of the road. To achieve the most from a wilderness experience, try to plan your trip to take you farther in, to get off the beaten path to the less-used areas.

The high, rugged peaks and long valleys provide a lifetime of recreation opportunities. The Wilderness is also home to many plants and animals and serves both as a refuge for species that are sensitive to human intrusion and as a reminder of what pre-European North America was like.

Trail Information

This guidebook describes the trailheads and major trails of the High Uintas Wilderness. Some nearby non-designated areas contain the same recreational, scenic and biological values as the official Wilderness and these areas were included too.

The trails are organized into a "tree and branch" structure starting from the major trailheads accessible with a passenger car. The "trunk" trail from the trailhead is described first followed by the various side, loop, and east-to-west trails that branch from the main trail. At the watershed divide the reader is referred to the next trailhead for the continuation.

Finding your own way is part of the Wilderness experience. The descriptions will help you select a destination and plan a trip and will get you to the trailhead. Forest service guidelines minimize the number of signs inside the Wilderness so do not expect a sign with mileage at every junction. Likewise, this book does not mention every stream crossing, trail junction, and landmark. Once on the trail you will need to use a map, your own on-the-ground observations, and common sense.

The main trails are heavily used by hikers and horses (and sometimes by sheep), so there is a well-defined track on the ground. But even popular trails can disappear in open grassy areas or in wet areas. In these cases you need to watch for blazes and rock cairns and look for the trail again on the far side. The popular lake basins are filled with informal tracks created by anglers, by campers, and by game and you have to search for the main route.

Finding off-trail lakes, bushwhacking up trailless side drainages, and scrambling onto the high ridges and plateaus require orienteering skill. Most casual off-trail exploration in the Uintas is done near timberline where distant views make route planning much easier than down in the timber.

Administrative Policies

The High Uintas is administered by two National Forests and includes trailheads in seven ranger districts. Office addresses and phone numbers are listed in the Appendix. The staff will try to answer your questions and are very good with general information. But this is a big area and the most knowledgeable individuals, the Wilderness rangers, are seldom in the office. Do not be surprised when the person answering the phone cannot tell you details about a particular trail. Besides, discovery is part of the Wilderness experience.

Permits are not required to visit the High Uintas Wilderness and this freedom can continue only if all users minimize their impact. There are self-service registration boxes at most trailheads. Every party should fill out a card as this gives the Forest Service valuable data in monitoring usage. The registration card is valuable if the rangers are asked to look for an overdue party, so filling out the card is for your own safety too.

Specific regulations to protect Wilderness are listed elsewhere. These rules are the result of trying to balance protecting the land with providing a high quality recreation experience.

Maps

The maps in this book are illustrations that show the relative position of trails and lakes to one another. They show both official trails and major cross-country routes mentioned in the text. The Wilderness boundary was deliberately not shown since the natural wilderness values begin at the trailhead, not at a political line. These sketch maps are all right if you have good trail sense or plan to stay on the main trails. Most visitors will want additional maps.

The High Uintas Wilderness Map produced by the Forest Service is available for $3.00 from any of the Forest Service offices in the area. Direct mail orders to the Forest Supervisor's Office in Salt Lake (Wasatch) or Vernal (Ashley). This map is very accurate and is a real bargain. It shows all the official trails and has topography and vegetation patterns as well. For easy cross reference, the administrative trail numbers that appear on this map are included in the heading of each trail description in this book. Sometimes a logical route on the ground consists of parts of several official Forest Service trail numbers.

The USGS topographic maps give the most detailed information for backcountry navigation and are highly recommended if off-trail routes are planned. The maps covering the Uintas are based on field work from the mid 1960's so the road and trail information is out of date but streams and mountains do not move. Topographic maps are available from many outdoor shops around Utah, from the Geological Survey Office in the Federal Building in Salt Lake City, or by mail for $2.50 each from the U.S. Geological Survey, Federal Center, Denver, Colorado 80225.

The Natural Environment

Hiking, photography, and nature-watching opportunities are defined by the land. A brief overview of the geography and ecological communities of the Uintas will aid in planning your trip.

Streams and glaciers have sculpted the Uintas uplift into the canyons and peaks of today. The North Slope drainages have the classic "U" shape of glacier-carved valleys. Lakes are common in the cirques at the heads of the drainages. Extensive bottomlands with a stream meandering through glacier-deposited rocky soil are walled in by long cliffs towering along both sides. The alternating hard and soft layers of the Precambrian rocks found in the center of the range tend to erode into spectacular cliffs with hundreds of feet of talus and boulders lying at the base. In a few areas the erosion has cut all the way to the divide leaving rugged knife-edge ridges that are difficult to cross and nearly impossible to travel along.

On the south and east of the Uintas the erosion of the uplift is far from complete. There are extensive areas of flat-topped mountains forming high-altitude plateaus between the drainages. The drainages tend to be wide and branching with intermediate ridges. There was less recent glacial activity on the South Slope and the major streams have cut V-shaped gorges and now flow far below the surrounding bench lands.

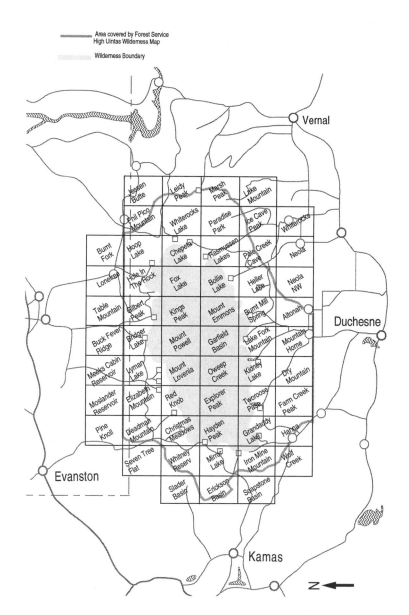

Area covered by Forest Service
High Uintas Wilderness Map

Wilderness Boundary

Vernal

Jessen Butte · Leidy Peak · Marsh Peak · Lake Mountain

Phil Pico Mountain · Whiterocks Lake · Paradise Park · Ice Cave Peak · Whiterocks

Burnt Fork · Hoop Lake · Chepeta Lake · Rasmussen Lakes · Pole Creek Cave · Neola

Lonetree · Hole In The Rock · Fox Lake · Bollie Lake · Heller Lake · Neola NW

Table Mountain · Gilbert Peak · Kings Peak · Mount Emmons · Burnt Mill Spring · Altonah

Buck Fever Ridge · Bridger Lake · Mount Powell · Garfield Basin · Lake Fork Mountain · Mountain Home

Meeks Cabin Reservoir · Wyman Lake · Mount Lovenia · Oweep Creek · Kidney Lake · Dry Mountain

Moslander Reservoir · Elizabeth Mountain · Red Knob · Explorer Peak · Twooroose Pass · Farm Creek Peak

Pine Knoll · Deadman Mountain · Christmas Meadows · Hayden Peak · Grandaddy Lake · Hanna

Seven Tree Flat · Whitney Reserv · Mirror Lake · Iron Mine Mountain · Wolf Creek

Slader Basin · Erickson Basin · Soapstone Basin

Duchesne

Evanston

Kamas

N

Key To Topographic Maps

Visitors to the North Slope drainages generally travel up along the main stream and return the same way or else exit the drainage at a well defined pass. On the South Slope the trails tend to follow the bench lands rather than the streams and the branching drainages create more opportunities for loop hikes.

The flat-topped ridges provide a unique hiking experience. Some ridges can be reached by an easy walk while others require several hours of steep off-trail scrambling up a boulder-covered slope. Once on top you can travel for miles going cross country through open tundra with spectacular views in every direction. There are many named summits with elevations over 12,000 feet along these flat-topped ridges.

None of the summits in the Wilderness have a maintained trail to the top but many can be reached by the average hiker. Some major summits, such as Brown Duck Mountain, can be reached simply by hiking up from the nearby trail following the crest of a wide ridge. Other summits, such as Kings Peak, require easy scrambling along a rocky crest to reach the summit. A few require careful route planning to find the safe scrambling route up through cliffs. Scrambling consists of climbing where you use your arms for balance but do not have to pull yourself up by your arms. A practical definition is that if your dog can follow the route it is scrambling and not technical climbing.

The Uintas have very few technical rock climbing routes. Generally if a cliff is steep enough to require roped climbing it has so much loose rock as to be unpleasant and objectively unsafe.

Seasons and Weather

The Uintas are high, cold, and wet—a striking contrast with the valleys and deserts of Utah. In June visitors will still encounter the lingering winter snow but most trails and passes are open by the beginning of July. In wet years, patches of snow survive through August on north-facing slopes above 12,000 feet. Night-time temperatures can drop to near freezing even during the summer.

Mountains create their own climate and rain clouds form as winds push over the high ridges. Driving across Wyoming on I-80 you can usually look south and see a wall of dark clouds hanging over the Uintas. Afternoon thunderstorms are common, especially on hot days. It can even snow in the Uintas any month of the year but these summer snowstorms usually melt off in a few hours.

The wet alpine weather creates the snow-frosted peaks, rushing streams, and dense forests that we all seek in the mountains. Be prepared for rain and snow and enjoy it as part of the Wilderness experience.

Plant Communities

The Uinta foothills are rolling sage-covered ridges which change progressively to pinyon-juniper and then to aspen forest as the access roads gain elevation. Higher up on the National Forest land the aspen gives way to conifer forest. The extensive park-like stands of lodgepole pine intermixed with areas of spruce-fir forest dominate the middle slopes. The forest band around the mountains extends from about 7000 to 10,000 foot elevation. Between 10,000 and 10,500 feet the trees start to thin out and grassy meadows become more frequent.

Timberline tends to be around 11,000 feet although trees survive higher up if they are in sheltered areas. Above timberline there are areas of low-growing brush alternating with grassy tundra areas. The Uintas have large areas of true alpine tundra and are typical of the Northern Rocky Mountains ecosystem.

Wildlife

The area is still home to most of the species that were there when Europeans arrived. Large mammals such as deer, elk, and moose are frequently seen, especially in the highly productive riparian areas. Beaver ponds are common. The Uintas are especially important as habitat for species which require large areas free from human disturbance. Black bear still wander the range. A reintroduced herd of Rocky Mountain bighorn sheep seems to be maintaining its population. Species dependent on old-growth forest such as the boreal owl, pine marten, and wolverine are surviving in the Wilderness but the magnificent wolf and grizzly bear competed with agriculture and are gone (for now).

Although the High Uintas Wilderness is large, it is not an isolated ecosystem. The populations of large mammals depend on winter range conditions down in the foothills and the populations of songbirds depend on winter range in Central and South America. To protect a local area we must think globally.

Fish

Fishing has long been a popular activity in the Uintas. The growth of fish is slow in the cold mountain lakes and fishing pressure, especially in the popular basins, is heavy. Many anglers are concluding that "a trout is too valuable to catch only once" and are emphasizing "catch and release" fishing. This preserves the challenge of the sport but improves the opportunities for those who come next week or next season.

Many lakes have been regularly stocked with rainbow, cutthroat, and eastern brook trout as well as the California golden trout and arctic grayling. In some lakes the heavy fishing pressure exceeds the ability of the population to recover. In other lakes overstocking has resulted in small stunted fish. Some introduced species are unable to reproduce in many lake basins due to unfavorable local conditions. The shallow lakes periodically freeze to the bottom and will have fish only if they have been recently restocked. The Utah Division of Wildlife Resources currently does aerial restocking of lakes on about a 3 to 5 year cycle.

Aerial fish stocking of Wilderness mountain lakes is controversial. The deeper lakes and streams once had healthy self-reproducing populations of native Colorado Basin and Bonneville cutthroat trout which have been eliminated by competition and hybridization with introduced fish. More importantly, many high-altitude lakes were naturally fish-free and introducing exotic fish endangers the native populations of small amphibians, crustaceans, insects, and aquatic plants.

The Wilderness is Federally protected but fish and wildlife are under state jurisdiction. The future of aerial stocking will involve balancing the desire to provide a recreational experience against the desire to allow Wilderness areas to be governed by natural processes.

Further Reading

This is a guidebook, not a text book, and the interested reader is referred to the references listed in the appendix for more detailed information on the geology, biology, history, and administration of the Uintas.

Access Roads

A Wilderness trip begins and ends at a road. The major forest roads are well-maintained gravel and a few are even paved. All the major trailheads in the Uintas can be reached by passenger car but some of the minor access point are on primitive roads that require a high-clearance vehicle or four-wheel-drive (4WD). All this assumes of course that the road is snow-free and that there have not been unusually heavy rain storms recently. Match your planned access point to the capability of your vehicle.

The trailhead descriptions include road conditions. If the description says the unpaved road is suitable for passenger cars it means that the road is occasionally graded and can be traveled by any standard highway vehicle. Typical speed on these gravel roads is 20 to 30 mph. If the description includes the qualifier "carefully driven passenger car" it means that the road is rough and has occasional ruts or oversized rocks. There may be some short sections where you will want to slow down, look ahead, and shift into first gear before proceeding.

Some trailheads are at the end of a primitive forest road and a pickup truck or similar high-clearance vehicle with low gears is advised due to steepness, large loose rocks, deep ruts, mud, stream fords or similar difficulties.

Most of these these primitive roads are not essential for wilderness access. Someone with a passenger car can park before the road really gets bad and simply walk the last mile or so of rough road to the end (for example, at Chepeta Lake or at the West Fork of Blacks Fork).

The Uintas are a big area. Standard highway maps do not clearly show the unpaved roads that lead to the trailheads. Some maps, such as the High Uintas Wilderness Map, show the roads near the trailheads but do not have enough paper to reach out to the main highways. The regional Ashley and Wasatch-Cache National Forest maps show every branch and spur road but do not always indicate which is the main route. The Uintas Area Road Map, page 27, shows the major recreation access routes and this section is an attempt to guide the visitor to the trailheads.

The Beltway

The Uintas are ringed by US 189, Utah 32, Interstate 80, Wyoming 414, Utah 43, Utah 44, US 191, and US 40. These are major all-season highways found on all road maps. The beltway generally stays 30 to 50 miles out from the mountains and connects the major towns: Heber, Kamas, Evanston, Mountain View, Vernal, Roosevelt, and Duchesne.

The trailhead descriptions give the most direct route from this beltway to the trailhead.

The Inner Highways

Closer to the mountains are a series of secondary state highways. The Mirror Lake Highway, numbered as Utah 150 and Wyoming 150, goes from Kamas, Utah to Evanston, Wyoming across a high pass at the western end of the Uintas. Utah 121, Utah 87, and Utah 35 east of Hanna are paved roads leading to small towns, homes and farms and stay outside the National Forest.

These inner highways are part of the route from the beltway to the forest roads going to the trailheads. These roads show on most highway maps and are generally well marked with signs.

Spur Roads

The pattern in the Uintas is that a main north and south road follows each major drainage past the last homes and farms and continues into the National Forest. These improved gravel roads are maintained by either the county, the Bureau of Indian Affairs, or the Forest Service. The roads can look confusing on the Forest Service maps with branches and loops going in every direction. But on the ground the roads are easy to follow, even when driving to the trailhead at night. The main road leading up a drainage is wider and better maintained and the side roads are clearly secondary. Conditions on gravel roads change during the course of a season. The condition mostly depends on how recently a grader smoothed out the washboard ridges and wheel ruts.

Connecting Roads

There is also a system of county and Forest Service roads, typically 1 to 10 miles out from the Wilderness and non-designated roadless areas, that makes a loop completely around the Uintas. These roads are mostly unpaved and some are only casually maintained but they are all passable to carefully driven passenger cars. These roads provide a useful shortcut between trailheads.

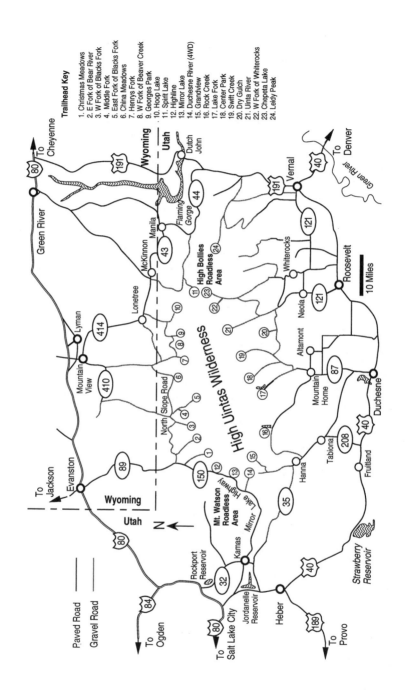

Trailhead Key

1. Christmas Meadows
2. E Fork of Bear River
3. W Fork of Blacks Fork
4. Middle Fork
5. East Fork of Blacks Fork
6. China Meadows
7. Henrys Fork
8. W Fork of Beaver Creek
9. Georges Park
10. Hoop Lake
11. Spirit Lake
12. Highline
13. Mirror Lake
14. Duchesne River (4WD)
15. Grandview
16. Rock Creek
17. Lake Fork
18. Center Park
19. Swift Creek
20. Dry Gulch
21. Uinta River
22. W Fork of Whiterocks
23. Chepeta Lake
24. Leidy Peak

Paved Road ——
Gravel Road ·····

27

They also offer access to worthwhile day hiking, sightseeing, and car camping outside the Wilderness.

The North Slope Road starts at the Mirror Lake highway, passes the West and East Forks of Blacks Fork and continues under various Forest Service road numbers to Smiths Fork, Henrys Fork and on to Hoop Lake then out to Wyoming 414 at Lonetree. Portions of this road are described in detail as part of the route to a particular trailhead but there is really a continuous road all the way. Another forest road runs from Wyoming 414 at McKinnon and goes past the Spirit Lake Road and ends on the scenic loop near Flaming Gorge.

On the South Slope there is a forest road going from Hanna to Stillwater Reservoir. Another series of forest roads leads east from the Yellowstone road to Uinta Canyon and on to the Chepeta Lake Road in the Whiterocks drainage. The Red Cloud Loop is a designated scenic byway that starts from Vernal and goes high onto the east end of the Uintas then back to Highway 191.

Indian Reservation Roads

Several access roads to the South Slope cross land belonging to the Uintah and Ouray Reservation. The main roads described in the trailhead descriptions are open to the public but the spur roads branching from the county road are marked with "Tribal Permission Required" signs. Stay on the main road and do not hike or camp until you are beyond the Ashley National Forest Boundary. Fishing on the Tribal land requires a tribal fishing license which can be obtained at many outdoor stores in the Uinta basin. Read the fishing proclamation for specific rules.

Primitive Roads

The multiple-use areas of the National Forest outside the Wilderness area are laced with roads cut for logging, grazing, and energy exploration. These are often only a bulldozer swath cut on native soil that was constructed for logging access. Most are open to vehicles, but consult the Forest Travel Plan if in doubt. Most recreational use of these primitive roads is by ATVs and mountain bikes in summer and by hunters equipped with 4WD in the fall. If you have a vehicle that can get there, these roads may be useful to reach a minor trail or a cross-country route into the Wilderness.

TIPS FOR THE WILDERNESS VISITOR

Backpacking is the most popular and economical way to get into the Wilderness. The heads of most Uinta drainages can be reached by two days of reasonable backpacking. The alternative, horses, is popular but expensive and involves more complex trip logistics.

Proper equipment, good physical condition, and careful planning are necessary for enjoyable backpacking. The most important items of equipment include good, comfortable footwear, your pack, sleeping bag, and tent or other shelter. There are many good books and magazine articles on modern backpacking techniques.

Menus for back country packing trips require careful planning. They must be simple but nutritious and substantial, and light in weight. Many basic dehydrated foods are available at any grocery store, and specialized items are found in sporting goods stores. Backpackers should be able to get by with 1 1/2 pounds (dry weight) of food per day. Don't count on catching and eating fish. If the fish are not biting, neither will you.

Minimum Impact Wilderness Travel

In the Wilderness, humans are temporary visitors. The Wilderness ideal is that the forces of nature should be allowed to dominate the land and the imprint of humans is substantially unnoticeable. The need for permits, visitor count restrictions, and other rules can be avoided if we all work toward having a minimum impact on the land. Wilderness visitors should behave responsibly, much as they would if visiting a church or the home of a respected friend.

Social Conduct

Solitude is an important part of the Wilderness experience. This means different things to different people, but it definitely includes freedom from the intrusion of unnatural sights and sounds. Respect the solitude by avoiding boisterous conduct and loud noises which are disruptive to others. Leave your radio at home or use an earphone. Camp well away from other parties, out earshot from other groups and, if possible, out of sight as well.

Large groups of people and large numbers of pack animals on the trail are disruptive to the experience of other Wilderness visitors. Large groups camping together tend to spread out onto less suitable areas and result in more vegetation damage and erosion. Limit your party size. Current regulations limit Wilderness party size to 14 but smaller groups are better. Consider splitting a large group and traveling as two independent parties.

Camping

There are two valid approaches to selecting a campsite to minimize impact: using already established sites and no-trace dispersed camping.

In heavily used areas there are already many informal campsites established by repeated use. Use an existing site where possible. Camping on an already disturbed site creates little additional impact.

When camping in more pristine areas select a site where you can achieve no-trace camping. That means avoiding fragile vegetation and easily eroded soils, moving your tent daily, and naturalizing the site when you leave. Nature will regenerate itself if given a chance.

The lake shores and streams are fragile areas. Set up camp at least 200 feet (75 paces) from lakes and streams to protect the biologically important area where water meets land.

Do not use soap or detergent in streams or lakes. Keep wash water, fish entrails, garbage and other trash well away from all bodies of water. Use a biodegradable soap and then use as little soap as possible. Disposing of cooking grease and soap is always a problem. One choice is to pour it into the ashes around the edge of a campfire. If you are not using a campfire, dig a hole, pour in the water, and replace the sod once the water has soaked in.

A gasoline or butane fueled camp stove is faster and more convenient than a wood fire for cooking. Using a stove is highly recommended as a way to protect the Wilderness. Trees grow slowly at high altitude and the most popular campsites are often near timberline. The result is shortage of firewood in many areas.

Above about 10,500 feet in the Uintas the limited wood is simply too valuable as part of the Wilderness to use it as fuel. Dead wood is an important part of the scenery and of the ecosystem. Save campfires for emergencies and for nights when you are camped at suitable, lower-elevation locations.

At lower altitudes and away from main trails the firewood is plentiful but visitors should still conserve it by keeping warming and cooking fires small. If you must build a fire, use an existing fire ring if available or else scatter the extinguished ashes and replace the sod when leaving. Do not build new fire rings. There are too many already.

Outdated practices such as trenching around tents, cutting boughs for bedding, cutting trees for "construction projects" and building roaring bonfires have no place in the heavily used Wilderness areas of today.

Anything you pack in you can pack out. Never bury your trash. Everything from orange peels to the foil from food packets should be packed out. Don't litter the trail. Put gum and candy wrappers and other similar material in your pocket while traveling. Everyone can help maintain a litter-free Wilderness by picking up trash which may have been thoughtlessly discarded by others.

Human Waste

There are no toilets in the back country. Fortunately, nature has provided a system of "biological disposers" that work to decompose feces. Keeping this in mind, you should:

1. Carry a small digging tool. A light garden trowel is good.

2. Select a suitable screened spot at least 200 feet from any stream or open water.

3. Dig a hole 8 to 10 inches in diameter, and no deeper than 6 to 8 inches - to stay within the "biological disposer" soil layer. Keep the sod intact if possible.

4. After use, fill the hole with loose soil and then tramp in the sod.

5. Toilet paper decomposes slowly, use a minimum. There is a trend toward packing it out. Others burn it—CAREFULLY.

Fire Hazard

Every visitor must be extremely cautious when using fire in any way. Smoking while traveling is forbidden, so be sure to stop in a safe place if you must smoke. Select a safe place to build your campfire. Never leave your fire until you are certain it is completely out and cold. When extinguishing your campfire, mix the hot coals with soil and water, stir it completely, and feel the ashes with your hands to be sure the coals are thoroughly cold.

In dry years there may be a total prohibition of fires outside developed campgrounds. Respect these fire closure orders for your own safety and for protection of the forest.

Axes, Guns, and Other Heavy Equipment

Leave them at home. Whether backpacking or horse packing there is no reason to carry heavy gear that you do not need. An excellent campfire can be made using only branches that are small enough, and dry enough, to break to length by hand.

Unless you are actually hunting, carrying a rifle is also unnecessary. There are other ways, such as simply backing away, to deal with bears and rattlesnakes. Listening to nearby target practice or encountering someone on the trail who is packing a hip pistol is an uncomfortable experience for most visitors.

Consider Using the Wilderness Less

One sure way to reduce your impact on the Wilderness is to use it less or to use it in less intrusive ways. Day hiking has less impact than camping. Backpacking has less impact than horse packing. Going to bed early has less impact than building a campfire. Nature observation has less impact than hunting and fishing.

There are many recreational opportunities available on the adjacent multiple-use forest areas. Activities such as mountain biking, car camping, and large groups are officially excluded from the Wilderness but are allowed and encouraged on other National Forest lands. But even for activities that are allowed in the Wilderness such as hiking, hunting, and photography, visitors should consider the possibility of using non-Wilderness lands.

Consider combining your Wilderness visit with activities out in the multiple-use area. For example, consider car camping along a primitive road and day hiking into the Wilderness rather than doing a short backpack to the overused lake nearest the trailhead. Or plan a large group social campfire evening outside the Wilderness at the start of the trip, then break into smaller groups for a few days of "no fires" backpacking.

For social, biological, and administrative reasons the non-Wilderness areas near the roads have a far greater human carrying capacity. These areas are at lower elevation and the longer season means the forest can recover more quickly. Human intrusions such as fisheries management and site reconstruction are more compatible with the non-Wilderness areas.

The Wilderness is a special place. If you want a Wilderness experience then go there. But consider visiting other public lands if you simply want an outdoor experience or do not want to reduce your impact to the level appropriate for Wilderness.

Personal Safety

This guidebook describes routes and assumes that the reader has the appropriate health, equipment, and level of skill to deal with the natural environment. Enjoy the adventures of a Wilderness experience, but do not take unnecessary chances. An illness or injury that is normally minor can become serious at high elevations. If you get sick, try to get out of the mountains, or at least to a lower elevation, while you can still travel.

Get in shape by taking long walks and short weekend hikes with a full pack. Even then, take it easy the first day or two. Most of this area is above 10,000 feet. High elevations may cause "altitude sickness" because there is less oxygen in the air. Walk slowly and steadily, and from time to time eat some candy or other quick energy food.

Leave word with friends where you are going and when you expect to return. Take a detailed map with you. It is never wise to travel alone, but if you must, be extra careful. If you think you are lost, take it easy, keep calm and don't panic. Sit down and try to figure out where you are. Use your head, not your legs.

Never go without rain gear. Sudden mountain storms are common, and there will probably be a thundershower every afternoon. Plan your day to cross ridges or climb summits in the morning or be prepared to wait out a storm before proceeding. During lightning storms, stay off ridges and peaks and away from open meadows and isolated trees. If possible, find shelter among dense, small trees in low areas. If this is not possible, squat down on top of a low flat rock or on your pack so you will not be a path for ground currents if lightning strikes nearby.

Also carry a warm jacket even in the middle of summer, as the temperature seldom gets above 70 degrees during the day and it frosts or freezes almost every night. Consult books on backpacking and wilderness travel for equipment and supplies checklists .

Stream Crossings

There are few bridges in the Wilderness area and many trails cross streams that are too wide to jump across. Trails that were originally constructed for horses are notorious for frequent stream crossings since they follow the side with the easiest terrain and horses walk across easily. Other trails cross wet muddy meadows and boggy areas. Wet boots are unpleasant and will cause blisters and cold feet. . Crossing streams barefoot with a full pack is painful and submerged sharp rocks and sticks can be dangerous.

A pair of sneakers aids in fording Uinta streams. John Veranth Photo

The best solution is to carry a pair of sneakers or sandals for the wet crossings. It takes only a few minutes on the other side to dry your feet and replace your boots. Your feet will be much more comfortable for the effort. The sneakers are also useful for crossing muddy sections of wet trail.

Water Treatment

All surface water is potentially contaminated with fecal matter. Humans, domestic livestock, and wild animals are all carriers of "bugs" that can cause disease. Carrying water is impractical for anything over a day hike so an effective treatment method is necessary.

Boiling, filters, and chemical treatments all have their disadvantages. Boiling is the most certain but requires time, especially at high altitude, and much fuel. Filters are heavy and slow. Chemical treatments have storage problems and are not 100% reliable, especially in cold water.

A reasonable approach is to select the water from the cleanest source possible, for instance snowmelt or a small spring above the trail rather than from a heavily used lake, then treat the water. Carry one high efficiency filter (such as First Need® or Katadyne®) for the party and fill water bottles in the morning and evening. At breakfast and dinner you will be boiling water anyway so this is an alternative. Carry iodine tablets (better shelf life than chlorine tablets, less messy than iodine crystals) to use if your water runs low while on the trail.

Trail Signs vs Landmark Navigation

Most trailheads have a large signboard with destinations, mileages, and sometimes maps. These help get you started but the Forest Service guidelines call for minimizing signs within Wilderness Areas. Geographic features are not marked and trail junction signs are small, list only one or two destinations, and are usually unpainted. The inconspicuous Wilderness trail signs are easy to miss. If you see a trail sign, be grateful and use the information but do not depend on signs.

Carry a good map of the area you will be traveling. Keep track of landmarks such as prominent peaks and stream crossings.

Your watch is as valuable as your compass for navigation. You can estimate your position if you know your pace. A typical hiker will average 2 1/2 miles per hour on forest trails plus 1/2 hour for every 1000 feet of elevation gain. So, for example, if you left a known point such as a trail junction one and a half hours ago and have been climbing gradually you can be reasonably sure you are about 3 miles and definitely less than 4 miles from your previous landmark.

Brown Duck Basin on Memorial Day Weekend / Dave Wallace Photo.

THE HIGH UINTAS -
Winter and Spring

The snow-free season in the High Uintas is only from July to September and for the other nine months of the year these mountains are largely unvisited. Experienced cross-country skiers should consider a winter or spring visit. There is a special sense of peace and solitude in the Uintas during these months.

The snow-covered open basins and ridges at the higher elevations are a mountaineer's delight. The ridges and summits look especially awesome when shrouded in snow. Cross-country ski travel is unimpeded by brush, boulder hopping, or boggy areas. It is possible to go for miles along the high ridges and then make an exciting descent down untracked slopes back to your camp.

A surprising number of skiers do mid-winter camping trips, and some even attempt Kings Peak ascents over the year-end holidays. But the best time for ski trips is from March through May and some years even into June. The days are longer and the snow has consolidated, making trail breaking far easier.

Winter approaches to the Uintas are long. A solution is to tow a sled when skiing across the flat terrain at the beginning and end. Inexpensive plastic sleds are an almost perfect fit for carrying a backpack.

Feasible ski backpack destinations are limited by the lack of winter road access to the higher elevations. It is no fun to spend the first day and last day of a trip hiking or skiing on marginal snow across the 10 or 15 miles from the end of the plowed road to the good snow.

Winter Access Points

There are a few places with good winter access. Since these roads are plowed primarily for access to an energy project or to private property, parking at the end may be difficult. Bring some big sturdy shovels and be prepared to carve a space if necessary to get your car completely off the road.

The best winter access is at Henrys Fork. The road from Lone Tree is plowed as far as a producing oil field only 3 miles north of the summer trailhead. The high starting elevation assures good skiing right from the car.

The road to Rock Creek is currently plowed to the Upper Stillwater Dam, a mile from the summer trailhead.

The Yellowstone Road is plowed by the county as far as Yellowstone Ranch which gets you within 4 miles of the Wilderness boundary and also gives access to the Hells Canyon Road.

The Mirror Lake Highway is plowed to a large snowmobile trailhead near the forest boundary south of Evanston. From here it is feasible to ski to the East Fork of the Bear River, to the Christmas Meadows area, or to Hell Hole Lake.

Spring Access

As spring approaches there are some additional options. The trick is to plan a trip after the road to the trailhead is plowed or melts open but before the snow vanishes from the backcountry.

The road to Moon Lake is closed for part of the winter but is plowed open fairly early in the spring and you can usually drive to the Moon Lake Campground by May 15. Since the trail gains elevation quickly there is usually good snow remaining in the Brown Duck Lake area that can be reached by a short wet hike up the trail from Moon Lake.

LeConte Lake in Early June
Dave WallacePhoto

The Mirror Lake Highway is plowed open in the spring so there is often a window of opportunity to drive to the Highline Trailhead while there is still excellent snow in the backcountry. The road is usually open over Bald Mountain Pass by Memorial Day. The best strategy is to call the highway department in the spring and check the road status.

The road to the East Fork of Blacks Fork Trailhead is usually open by June 1 and there still may be good snow up on the Bald Mountain route to Smiths Fork at that time.

Wilderness Regulations

The Forest Service has issued certain regulations to protect the Wilderness. When planning your trip be aware that the following are **PROHIBITED** within the High Uintas Wilderness.

1. Group size exceeding 14 persons and 15 head of stock.

2. Terrain permitting, camping within 200 feet of trails, lakes, ponds, springs and other water sources.

3. Camping within 100 feet of an occupied campsite.

4. Camping for more than 14 days at an individual site

5. Shortcutting a trail switchback.

6. Disposing of debris, garbage or other waste. (Human waste and food scraps must be buried; all other garbage, debris and waste must be packed out of the Wilderness.)

7. Bedding, tethering, hobbling, or hitching a horse or other saddle or pack animal overnight within 200 feet of lakes or springs.

Camping near Amethyst Lake / Dave Wallace Photo

THE NORTH SLOPE

Introduction

The upper basins of the glacier-carved North Slope drainages have the most rugged alpine scenery in the High Uintas. The remnants of glacial activity are everywhere. The valleys have a classic "U" shape with flat bottom land and steep walls along the sides. Lateral and terminal moraines form rocky ridges. Deep, round lakes are found in the cirques at the heads of the drainages. Throughout the Wilderness the country is all fairly rocky. There may be some smooth dirt trails at lower elevations but in the upper areas there is little soil.

The headwaters of the East Fork of the Bear River and the three branches of Blacks Fork have the most rugged peaks. Many of the ridges are nearly impossible to travel along due to cliffs and intermediate summits. The passes across the rugged knife-edge ridges on the Uinta crest are difficult but hikers can exit from any of the North Slope drainages and reach the headwater basins along the long South Slope.

Stillwater Fork (Christmas Meadows Trailhead), Henrys Fork and the Red Castle (Smiths Fork) are the most heavily used lake basins on the North Slope. But other drainages on the North Slope are just as attractive and those seeking a true wilderness experience can explore away from the highly used areas. East of Henrys Fork the country remains at a high elevation but ridges become more rounded and drainages are less visited.

The North Slope is heavily grazed by cattle and sheep. The Forest Service is responsible for managing grazing on the various allotments. They rotate grazing areas so they will not always be in the same place. Most of the sheep on both the North and South Slopes are driven onto the National Forest land following the East Fork of Blacks Fork and then they fan out into the various drainages. Most of the main lakes are closed to sheep. However, the flocks wander where they want and not just where permitted.

Christmas Meadows Trailhead

Destination	Miles One Way	Elevation Gain
Wilderness Boundary	2 1/2	200
Amethyst Lake	6	2000
Kermsuh Lake	7	1500
Ryder Lake	8	1900

USGS Maps: Christmas Meadows, Hayden Peak

A trail goes up the Stillwater Fork of the Bear River and branches to reach several beautiful lakes along the Uinta crest. Amethyst Lake is the largest in this drainage. Other large lakes include Ostler, Kermsuh, Ryder, and McPheters. The trail starts fairly low and you begin hiking in aspen which changes to spruce and pine as you gain elevation. The lakes are near timberline with open meadows providing unobstructed views of the rocky ridges above. This is a popular trailhead since it is close to Salt Lake City and the drainages are short enough for you to camp near the top on even a two-day backpack.

To get to Christmas Meadows take the Mirror Lake Highway to the turnoff which is about 46 miles northeast of Kamas and 30 miles south of Evanston. Here, just north of the Stillwater Campground, an improved gravel road goes east then south about 4 miles along the Stillwater Fork to the Christmas Meadows Campground. This is a very popular camping area located along the stream in the timber. At the upper end of the campground a spur road continues to the trailhead. There is a recently reconstructed parking lot for cars and horse trailers with modern facilities, picnic tables and a signboard.

Stillwater Trail (#098)

The trail starts as a well defined and heavily used path following the stream. About 4 miles from the trailhead you come to a fork. The left branch goes to Ostler and Amethyst Lakes and the right fork is the Stillwater Trail going to the Ryder Lake area.

About 2 miles farther south on the Stillwater Trail, you reach another junction. Here, the west branch goes to Kermsuh Lake.

Continuing south from the Kermsuh Lake junction you will have a fairly rugged climb over a well-marked trail until you get out of the canyon and onto the more level country in the upper bowl. Here you will pass through open meadows to Ryder Lake. Both Ryder and McPheters Lakes are fairly large (about 25 acres), and sit in glacial cirques near the crest of the Uinta Mountains. McPheters Lake sits about 1/2 mile north of Ryder Lake, on a higher shelf at the base of Hayden Peak.

Hayden Peak, Mount Agassiz, Spread Eagle Peak and Ostler Peak ring the upper basin of the Stillwater Fork. There are over two dozen lakes and ponds in this basin and most have fishing. There is plenty of room to camp, so if you want to get away from other campers look around for another site. There is plenty of room but be sure to stay at least 200 feet from the lakes.

Ryder Lake
Utah Division of Wildlife Resources Photo

Branch Trails from the Stillwater Trail

Kermsuh Lake Trail (#139)

From the starting junction on the Stillwater Trail, you climb steep switchbacks to get out of the canyon, then level off into meadows below Hayden Peak. Kermsuh Lake (12 acres) lies at the head of the basin, just across the ridge from McPheters and Ryder Lakes. It is a very pretty lake but has variable fishing success since it is not stocked. It is a nice place for camping—not too crowded. The best camping is in the meadows 1/2 mile below the outlet.

The upper basin is ringed by glacier-sculpted walls with Hayden Peak rising 2000 feet above the lake. You can scramble across the pass to reach the Hell Hole area to the south. Kletting and A-1 peaks are directly south but these peaks are more commonly climbed from the opposite side.

Off-trail Routes from Stillwater Fork

Starting half way between the Kermsuh Lake junction and Ryder Lake, you can bushwhack cross-country and climb the ridge just northeast of Spread Eagle Peak. From here the scrambling continues east then north along the ridge toward Ostler Peak or southwest to Spread Eagle

Mount Agassiz summit can be reached by steep off-trail hiking up the boulder-covered ridge above Ryder Lake. This is a wide and open slope so you can pick out your route from a distance.

McPheters Lake is only 2 miles from the Highline Trailhead across the ridge. The crossing involves scrambling and picking your way through the cliffs on the McPheters Lake side. This route is described from the Highline Trailhead.

Amethyst Lake Trail (#149)

This trail goes east to Ostler and Amethyst Lakes. At the Ostler Fork junction you turn left (east) up Ostler Creek. The first 2 miles of this trail are quite steep and rocky and are well marked but somewhat washed out. The trail levels off and becomes more pleasant as you start passing through meadows mixed with spruce forest. The favorite camping spot on this trail is almost due east of Ostler Lake on a terminal moraine at the north end of a large meadow. Most campers stay here because it's about the last place with protection from the weather. This isn't above timberline, but the forest gets open and scrubby above here.

From the camping spot, the trail goes across to the west side of the meadow, ascending and swinging to the right, and continues on to Amethyst Lake. This is a large lake of 42 acres, surrounded by rock slides and cliffs. There are some scrubby spruce around the lower end where you could camp, but the campsites are more exposed to the weather than lower down in the heavier timber. This is one of the better fishing lakes in the Uintas, but it gets more use than others in the basin. The trail ends near Amethyst Lake but you are near the end of the basin and there is no way you can get lost here.

Ostler Lake
Utah Wildlife Resources Photo

Off-trail Routes from Amethyst Lake

From the camping spot on the moraine, Ostler Lake lies due west about 1/2 mile, but there is no trail to it. To get there, just climb up through the timber to the west and you'll find it at the base of a rock slide. It has fishing for brook and cutthroat trout and has some small, rocky campsites on the southwest end.

Salamander and Toomset lakes are above the trail along the base of the ridge running north from Ostler Peak. These lakes are in the trees, not in open country. There is no trail and finding the lakes is a satisfying exercise in orienteering. These are scenic lakes that are worth visiting on a day hike, especially if you are looking for solitude, but these lakes have poor campsites.

Ostler Peak

To reach Ostler Peak from Ostler Lake continue up the ridge from the lake. There are some boulder hopping and rockslides so plan your route carefully. The route up Ostler Peak from the Rock Creek drainage is probably easier.

45

Hell Hole Lake
(Main Fork of Stillwater)

The lower portion of this drainage is roadless but outside the Wilderness boundary. Higher up is a delightful lake, just inside the Wilderness, and above the lake are off-trail hiking routes. The area is easy to reach from the highway but is lightly used. Oil exploration is proposed for the area and access conditions are subject to sudden change.

About 2 1/2 miles south of the Christmas Meadows road turnoff a 4WD road branches east from the Mirror Lake Highway. It fords the Hayden Fork of the Bear River and goes southeast around the edge of a ridge to enter the drainage coming down from Hell Hole Lake. About 2 1/4 miles from the start there is a second stream crossing. A trail continues up along the east side of the river for 3 1/2 more miles, ascends one last rise and ends at Hell Hole Lake. The area around the lake contains boggy meadows and thick patches of conifers with excellent campsites. From the lake there are clear views of the rocky ridges above.

Off-trail hiking continues above the lakes. You can cross the pass and reach the Kermsuh Lake basin on the other side or you can follow the ridge to the summit of Kletting Peak. From Kletting Peak you can look north back down the Main Stillwater drainage and south past Kermsuh Lake and deeper into the Wilderness. The view is worth the effort.

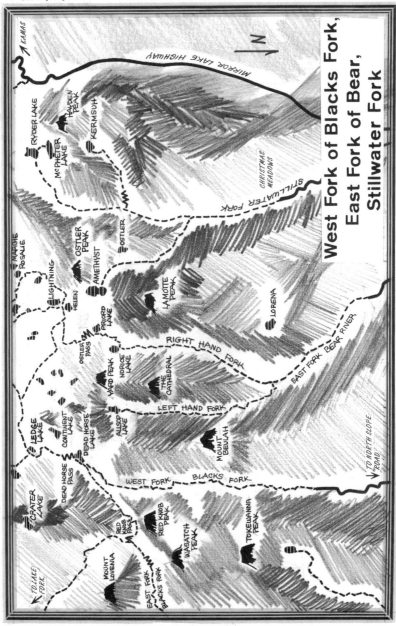

West Fork of Blacks Fork, East Fork of Bear, Stillwater Fork

East Fork of Bear River Trailhead

Destination	Miles One Way	Elevation Gain
Wilderness Boundary	3 1/2	140
Norice Lake	8 1/2	1440
Priord Lake	9 1/2	1840
Allsop Lake	8 1/2	1600
Ostler Pass	10	2600

USGS Maps: Christmas Meadows, Red Knob

The East Fork of the Bear is long drainage that splits into two major forks inside the Wilderness. Trails follow the streams all the way to the alpine lakes near the main Uinta crest. Both the trail up the East Fork and the west-to-east Bear River-Smiths Fork trail leave from this trailhead.

Dense willows on either side of the stream provide good habitat for moose which may be seen best in the early morning or late afternoon. The area is near a Boy Scout camp and scout groups are frequent summer visitors in the backcountry.

To get to the trailhead take the Mirror Lake Highway to the turnoff, 49 miles northeast of Kamas and 29 miles south of Evanston. The North Slope Road is a wide but rough gravel road that starts just south of the Wasatch National Forest boundary sign. Turn east on the North Slope Road and go 1.7 miles then turn right (south) onto the East Fork Road. Continue south for 4 miles on a good gravel road to a junction where the right branch goes to the Boy Scout camp and the left fork goes to the trailhead. The road gets narrow and rough after the junction but is still suitable for cars. At the trailhead the road makes a loop and there is parking and a toilet. The actual trailhead is between the signboard and the horse unloading ramp. It is a well defined trail.

East Fork of Bear River Trail (#100)

The trail runs above the stream where, shortly after starting, you pass the old buildings from a tie-hack camp where ties were cut for the railroad. Continue south for 1 1/2 miles beyond the tie-hack camp to a trail junction near the Wilderness boundary. The left fork goes to Allsop Lake, the right to Norice and Priord Lakes.

Continuing south on the right hand fork of the trail, you are pretty much on the stream grade all the way and it's not a difficult hike. You will be down in the timber and it's not too scenic until you reach the higher elevations. The trail becomes intermittent and harder to follow as you approach Norice Lake. Norice is a small meadow lake of 5 acres with good camping places.

Just before reaching Norice Lake, the trail branches off to the right and climbs to reach Priord Lake in about a mile. Priord Lake has good campsites and sits in a beautiful glacial cirque below Ostler Pass.

Routes from the East Fork Trail

There is a very steep, rough off-trail route from Norice Lake going over the ridge to the east to Allsop Lake. Only experienced hikers should attempt it because of cliffs on the other side.

From Priord Lake, a route continues south, switching up to a pass in about a mile of steep climbing. It was once a trail but has been officially abandoned and has not been maintained for about 30 years. From the pass, the route descends to join the Head of Rock Creek Trail in about 1 1/2 miles, just east of Helen Lake.

Allsop Lake Trail (#151)

The left hand trail takes you to Allsop Lake. The trail follows the stream all the way, so it's not difficult hiking. This is a glacial lake sitting at the head of the basin against the crest of the Uintas. It has good campsites but campsites are better a mile or so downstream from the lake.

Off-trail Routes from Allsop Lake

From Allsop Lake experienced hikers can go southeast across the ridge and join the Highline Trail or the West Fork of Blacks Fork at Dead Horse Lake. There is no trail; you just strike off cross-country, heading for the low spot on the ridge to the southeast. The slope going up to the ridge is steep and rocky, but once you are on the ridge, it's a nice easy trip through very beautiful country down to Dead Horse Lake.

Lamotte Peak

Lamotte Peak can be approached from the East Fork of the Bear by going cross-country from the Priord Lake area. It can also be climbed from the Ostler Fork side. [Duke Moscon]

West Fork of Blacks Fork Trailhead

Destination	Miles One Way	Elevation Gain
Wilderness Boundary	3 1/2	250
Dead Horse Lake	10 1/2	1480
Dead Horse Pass	11 1/2	2200
Red Knob Pass	13	2600

USGS Maps: Elizabeth Mountain*, Red Knob, Explorer Peak

This trail leads through a mixture of forest and meadow along one of the prettiest streams you will find anywhere. The area along the stream is excellent wildlife habitat and sightings of birds, elk, and moose are common. The trail climbs gradually all the way to Dead Horse Lake then ascends the steep slope to the crest of the Uintas at Dead Horse Pass. The Highline Trail crosses Dead Horse Pass coming from the Rock Creek Drainage on the South Slope and continues for a short way through the upper Blacks Fork drainage before recrossing to the South Slope at Red Knob Pass.

The trail begins from the end of the road that heads south along the West Fork of Blacks Fork. To get there from the west, take the Mirror Lake Highway to the turnoff for the North Slope Road, 49 miles northeast of Kamas and 29 miles south of Evanston. Go on a gravel road for 20 miles over Elizabeth Pass and down to a T-junction near Lyman Lake. Between the start of the North Slope Road and this junction all side roads are clear turnoffs and the main route continues straight.

At the Lyman Lake junction the North Slope Road jogs 100 feet right to another T-junction. Here the road to the West Fork of Blacks Fork turns sharply right and goes back west following the stream. The left branch at the second junction continues east for 2.3 rough miles to join a good road coming south from Robertson, Wyoming. See the East Fork of Blacks Fork Trailhead for descriptions of this alternative route.

You can drive a passenger car up the West Fork road for 4 or 5 miles. Use care as it is an unimproved road. It goes up to a large open meadow along the stream. This stream is fished heavily. You will come to a major stream crossing with a good car camping spot in the edge of the timber just before the crossing. High-clearance and 4WD vehicles can cross but those with passenger cars should park here and walk the last 2 miles to the end of the primitive road. Hikers can cross on the sheep bridge that is a few hundred yards downstream.

The stream ford is not very deep but it can be treacherous because the bottom is gravel and shifting sand. You would not want to try it except in late summer. Even four-wheel drives have been stuck here, so take a close look before trying it.

Walk or drive up a primitive road for 3/4 mile to a big pole fence with a gate. Due to extremely bad road conditions and sensitive soils ahead, leaving even a 4WD vehicle here is recommended. In another 1/2 mile there is a trail sign where the Bear River-Smiths Fork Trail crosses. The way toward the West Fork Trail continues straight ahead a short way and then takes the left fork and follows the primitive road through another fence. The road ends at a trailhead sign about a mile beyond the Bear River-Smiths Fork Trail crossing.

West Fork of Blacks Fork Trail (#101)

There is actually a foot trail on both sides of the stream. From the second stream crossing near where the primitive road ends, the best marked and best maintained trail is on the west side of the stream. A footbridge has been constructed at the upper end of Buck Pasture. If you stay on the west side you can go most of the way up the drainage without having to cross the stream again. The route follows the stream so you cannot get lost and the meadows offer nice views of the high ridge lines on both sides. This is an easy, gentle trail along the stream until you get to within a couple of miles of the end, where you start climbing fairly rapidly.

When you get almost to the head of the drainage, there is a trail junction. Here you will join the Highline Trail which runs between Dead Horse Pass and Red Knob Pass. Continuing up the creek on the Highline Trail, you will reach Dead Horse Lake, which is a rocky glacial lake at 11,000 feet. Sitting against the base of Dead Horse Pass, this 16 acre emerald-green lake is well worth the trip for the scenic pleasure of being there. The area is near timberline and scree-covered slopes reach from the lake to the ridge.

There are campsites near the outlet of Dead Horse Lake. You could easily spend several days here exploring the upper basin of Blacks Fork and the nearby basins across the passes to the south. From the head of the West Fork you can easily reach three drainages: the East Fork of Blacks Fork, the Lake Fork drainage on the south, and upper Rock Creek, also on the south.

Highline Trail

To Dead Horse Pass

The trail up to Dead Horse Pass is rather hazardous. It is steep, rocky, and subject to rock slides and washouts. It climbs 1000 feet from the lake to cross the rugged crest of the Uintas. The ascent to the pass is above timberline, over steep talus slopes. Some sections cross shale deposits that can slide away in a big mud flow. A snowbank stays here very late some years, hindering access. Experienced hikers can pick their way through but sometimes horses cannot make it.

To Red Knob Pass

From the trail junction below Dead Horse Lake, you climb east on the Highline Trail to Red Knob Pass at 12,000 feet between Red Knob Peak and Mount Lovenia. Crossing through the pass and down a way, is a trail junction. The trail to the east traverses high on the mountain then crosses back to the north, down into the East Fork of Blacks Fork. The Highline Trail continues south down into the upper basin of the Lake Fork River.

Bear River - Smiths Fork Trail
From West Fork of Blacks Fork

On the primitive road between the first stream crossing and the end there is a sign indicating Dead Horse Lakes straight ahead and Smiths Fork Trail to the left and right. The east-to-west Smiths Fork to Bear River Trail crosses here and you can see a well traveled track to the left that leads east to the Middle Fork of Blacks Fork and continues to the East Fork of Blacks Fork Trailhead. To the right the Smiths Fork Trail is a little harder to find. You have to backtrack about 30-40 yards and ford the river. On the other side you will find a track and occasional blazes leading west to the East Fork of Bear River Trailhead.

This trail does not enter the Wilderness but it passes through some impressive roadless country. It travels across the drainages staying largely in heavy timber. The trail is used by sheepherders who move their flocks from the Blacks Fork area up onto summer grazing allotments. The trail is useful for a day hike and as a way to get back to your car if you make a loop hike between drainages. See the descriptions of the East and Middle Forks of Blacks Fork for additional information on this trail.

Middle Fork of Blacks Fork Access

Destination	Miles One Way	Elevation Gain
Bear River-Smiths Fork Trail	4 1/2	800
Wilderness Boundary	10	1800
Tokewanna Summit	12+	3800

USGS Maps: Lyman Lake, Mount Lovenia

The Blacks Fork River is fed by three glaciated valleys at its head. The West and East Forks of Blacks Fork are the major branches and extend deep into the Wilderness. The Middle Fork is shorter and ends below Tokewanna Peak. Only the uppermost basin of the Middle Fork is within the Wilderness Area. There are some small lakes at the head of the drainage with good camping places and little fishing pressure.

The land between the North Slope Road and the designated Wilderness boundary is still wild and natural but there is intense pressure for timber cutting and oil exploration and there are intense efforts by citizen groups trying to protect the area. It is well worth visiting — now.

The road access to the Middle Fork of Blacks Fork is from the road to the East Fork. Follow the East Fork directions to the junction of the North Slope Road with the road from Robertson. The East Fork Road heads south from this junction and crosses the river on a modern concrete bridge. A primitive road starts at an unmarked gate 0.1 mile south of the bridge and heads west then south for 2 1/2 miles to a road closure where it becomes a trail. The road is not maintained and passenger car drivers may want to stop early.

Middle Fork of Blacks Fork Trail (#096)

Beyond the road closure, a trail goes directly up the Middle Fork. Several miles up this trail is a very old dilapidated logging camp about a mile below the junction of the Middle Fork Trail and the Bear River-Smiths Fork Trail. Note: Due to proposed extractive projects, the road conditions in the Middle Fork may change radically in coming years.

The trail follows the west bank of the stream, enters the Wilderness, and ends in the basin at the foot of Tokewanna Peak. The lakes have pretty good fishing as the area is not much used. There is good camping ground the full distance along the Middle Fork Creek. It's an easy access to Tokewanna Peak.

Bear River - Smiths Fork Trail (#191)

You can also get into the Middle Fork from either the West Fork or the East Fork using the Bear River - Smiths Fork Trail.

From the West Fork, start by finding the junction between the stream crossing and the end of the primitive road. You cross the ridge, drop down onto the Middle Fork Trail, and continue south up into the basin.

The other way is to take the trail described from the East Fork of Blacks Fork Trailhead. The trail to the west climbs across the ridge and drops to join the Middle Fork Trail.

Tokewanna Peak Summit (Elevation 13,165)

The Middle Fork is the most popular access to Tokewanna Peak. From the upper basin it is a steep climb over an open grassy slope right to the top. This summit is well north of the main Uinta crest so you have excellent views along the entire range.

Tokewanna Peak from Bear River-Smiths Fork Trail
John Veranth Photo

East Fork of Blacks Fork Trailhead

Destination	Miles One Way	Elevation Gain
Wilderness Boundary	2 1/2	300
Timberline	8	1500
Red Knob Pass	11 1/2	2700
Squaw Pass	9	2500

USGS Maps: Lyman Lake, Mount Lovenia

This trail splits shortly after beginning; the left fork is the Little East Fork Trail and the right branch continues up the main East Fork. Both trails lead into the Wilderness and offer fishing lakes and streams and little-used camping places but the area is also heavily used as a sheep driveway. Most of the sheep that graze in the High Uintas enter and exit by being driven up Blacks Fork, then they fan out to the east, west, and south across the divide.

The East Fork Trail climbs to Red Knob Pass where you can cross over into the Lake Fork drainage to the south or into the West Fork of Blacks Fork. The Little East Fork Trail climbs to Squaw Pass which leads into Oweep Basin in the Lake Fork drainage. The loop going up one trail, across the upper Lake Fork drainage following the Highline Trail, and returning back down the other has been called the finest backpacking loop in the Uintas. The country is spectacular, the trails are easy to follow, and you end up right back at your car.

To get to the trailhead from the north, take I-80 east of Evanston to the Fort Bridger exit, then take the "I-80 Business Loop" that runs from Fort Bridger to Lyman. Go 3 miles east to a four-way intersection where you turn south to Mountain View. At Mountain View, 4.4 miles south of the four-way intersection, take Wyoming 410 west. After 5.8 more miles the paved road makes a bend west toward Robertson and the gravel road to China Meadows and Henrys Fork heads straight south. Stay on the paved road, go straight through Robertson and continue about 4 miles to a junction that is 16.6 miles from the four-way intersection. Here Wyoming 410 ends, Uinta County road 204 continues straight and Uinta County 271 turns left toward the Meeks Cabin and the East Fork Trailhead.

The pavement ends after another 1.7 miles and a well-maintained gravel road continues south through open sagebrush-covered ranchland. The Wasatch National Forest boundary is at the north end of the Meeks Cabin Reservoir, 12.9 miles south of the junction with Wyoming 410. At mile 18.1 the forest road toward Hewinta Guard Station and China Meadows branches east and the main road continues straight. The junction with the North Slope Road west toward Lyman Lake and the Mirror Lake Highway is at mile 18.8. The main road continues straight and crosses the concrete bridge just ahead and starts up the East Fork of Blacks Fork.

The trailhead parking is on the right, just inside the campground fence, at mile 24.2 from the end of Wyoming 410. This road is well maintained and is the best route for passenger cars. Overall it is 46 miles from I-80 to the trailhead.

If you are coming from the west, the North Slope road is a shorter but slower access. See the description for the West Fork of Blacks Fork for this route. It is 24 miles from the Mirror Lake Highway across the North Slope Road to the trailhead. The 2.6 miles from the West Fork turnoff to the bridge leading to the East Fork are rough but all right for carefully driven passenger cars.

East Fork of Blacks Fork Trail (#102)

The trail starts at a signboard near the entrance fence and crosses the stream on a foot bridge, then turns south. After about 20 minutes the trail enters a wet meadow and makes a sharp turn to the right, then continues into a second meadow. Here it meets a well-used horse trail that comes up the west side from the campground and fords the stream. The new foot trail through the meadow is marked by a couple of posts with trail arrow signs.

About 1/4 mile beyond the junction with the horse trail, in the middle of a meadow, the trail crosses the Little East Fork stream on a bridge. Just beyond is the trail junction. Both branch trails from here have a fairly obvious tread and are easy to follow.

Just beyond the ruins of a log cabin the East Fork Trail crosses the stream on a dilapidated bridge and continues south reaching the Wilderness Boundary in another mile.

The East Fork of Blacks Fork Trail is very level and goes up a broad valley with alternating meadow and lodgepole pine forest. This is an excellent area for seeing large herds of moose. There are nice views of Bald Mountain and of the ridges on each side and there are ample camping spots in the meadows. The trail follows the stream all the way to timberline in the upper basin, then climbs steeply up switchbacks a final mile to Red Knob Pass.

Little East Fork Trail (#103)

From the trail junction 1 1/2 miles from the trailhead, the Little East Fork Trail follows its stream all the way to the upper basin, then continues on up to Squaw Pass. The route ascends through the mixed conifer forest that is typical of the North Slope.

From Squaw Pass you can continue down to join the Highline Trail in Oweep Basin in the upper east side of the Lake Fork drainage. For the loop backpack, continue west to Red Knob Pass.

There are several small lakes set in small basins high on the side of the ridge above the trail about two-thirds of the way up the Little East Fork. These lakes are sparkling jewels surrounded by boulder slopes and patches of forest. Views are outstanding but campsites are limited. The lakes may be found by going west, following the larger streams to the lakes.

Unnamed Lake in the Little East Fork of Blacks Fork
Utah Division of Wildlife Resources Photo

Bear River - Smiths Fork Trail (#091)
Going West from East Fork of Blacks Fork

Destination	Miles One Way	Elevation Change
East Fork of Blacks Fork to Ridge	2 1/2	1300
Ridge to Middle Fork of Blacks Fork	2 1/4	-800
Middle Fork to West Ridge	1	500
Ridge to East Fork of Blacks Fork	3 1/2	-900

USGS Maps: Lyman Lake, Mount Powell

This trail offers an alternative access to the Middle Fork and to Tokewanna. The short hike from the road to the ridge top viewpoint is one of the best day hikes in the area and offers spectacular scenery for the effort.

To get to the trailhead see directions for the East Fork of Blacks Fork Trailhead. The Bear River-Smiths Fork Trail crosses the road 4.9 miles south of the bridge and 0.6 mile north of the campground. There is parking on the spur road to the east.

The westbound Bear River-Smiths Fork Trail starts as a wide straight cut through the trees heading straight up the hill. Within 1/2 mile it narrows to a trail that ascends the ridge in a series of switchbacks. There is a very obvious and well-maintained tread through the woods and it is marked with blazes. At the top, the ridge becomes very broad and the trail levels off.

There is an excellent viewpoint on the ridge crest in a meadow just to the north of the trail. Looking at the ridge toward Tokewanna and seeing much of the East and Middle Fork of Blacks Fork you can sense the majesty of the Uintas.

Tokewanna Peak from East Fork of Blacks Fork

A scenic alternative route to Tokewanna is to take the Bear River-Smiths Fork Trail up to the ridge crest, then go south on the ridge between the East and Middle Forks. Go for about a mile through forest on a compass bearing along a broad ridge. This brings you out onto an absolutely spectacular opening between the forks. You can hike for several more miles along a broad grass-covered plateau and continue up onto a spur ridge of Tokewanna to the summit.

Bald Mountain Route

Bear River - Smiths Fork Trail East from Blacks Fork (#091, #111)

Destination	Miles One Way	Elevation Gain
Wilderness Boundary	1 1/2	1100
Timberline	3	1500
Bald Mountain Ridge	4	2300
East Fork of Smiths Fork Trail	8	-800
Red Castle Lake	10 1/2	2800
Smiths Fork Pass	13 1/2	3000

USGS Maps: Mount Powell, Lyman Lake

The Bald Mountain route is a higher and more scenic approach to the Red Castle Lakes than coming up the direct trail from China Meadows. You are above timberline much of the way but the spectacular views have a price. The route has a steep climb up onto Bald Mountain at the beginning and involves 600 feet of elevation loss getting back down to the East Fork of Smiths Fork below Lower Red Castle Lake. The Bear River-Smiths Fork Trail crosses the drainage and goes past East Red Castle to Smiths Fork Pass.

To get to the trailhead see directions for the East Fork of Blacks Fork Trailhead. The Bald Mountain Trail leaves the road 4.9 miles south of the bridge and 0.6 mile north of the campground. There is parking on the spur road to the east. Go to the right of a gravel pit operation and down to the stream ford. A better start for hikers at high water is to go to the East Fork Trailhead, cross the foot bridge and then walk back downstream to rejoin the Bald Mountain Trail. A blazed trail leads north from the bridge and meets the Bear River-Smiths Fork Trail up the hill from the stream crossing.

From the river crossing you go east and it is a very steep climb for the next mile to the top. Here the trail forks and the North Slope Trail contours east while the route to Red Castle continues climbing to the south. This trail will take you around the east base of Bald Mountain above Bald Lake.

Continuing south the scenery is really nice all across the long open ridge. Then you switchback down from the ridge onto the bench above the East Fork of Smiths Fork. An unmaintained sheep trail splits off from the main trail at about 10,960 feet and follows the stream down to Broadbent Meadows. The trail toward Red Castle continues along the bench to the south to reach the junction with the direct trail. Continuing up, there is another fork where the west trail goes to Lower, Main, and Upper Red Castle Lakes. The east trail goes past East Red Castle Lake to Smiths Fork Pass.

Off-trail Routes from Bald Mountain Trail

There is no trail down to Bald Lake from the Bald Mountain Trail but you can see the lake from the trail and find your way down. It is a good fishing and camping place if you want to stop there.

Bald Mountain Summit can easily be reached by leaving the trail and hiking to the high point of the ridge.

Red Castle Peak above Lower Red Castle Lake / Thad Eagar Photo

China Meadows Trailhead

Destination	Miles One Way	Elevation Gain
Wilderness Boundary	3/4	
Bald Mtn Trail Junction	8 1/4	1200
Red Castle Lake	11	1800
Smiths Fork Pass	12 1/2	2300

USGS Maps: Bridger Lake, Mount Powell

This is the direct trail to the Red Castle Lakes, following the East Fork stream all the way. It is less scenic than the Bald Mountain route since you spend a lot of time down in thick forest but it avoids the steep climb at the beginning.

It is a modern trail, well reconstructed, with corduroy across the boggy spots, one of the best trails on the North Slope. Once into the Red Castle Basin area, stream fishing is good and scenery is excellent. The name comes from its outstanding feature, a large red-rock peak formed from sheer cliffs split by large fractures. When the light shines on it, it has an intense red, especially when reflected in the lake, and looks like a castle with spires. The lakes are still in timber country but where the forest is beginning to open up into parks. You don't run out of timber until you get to the ledge just below Upper Red Castle Lake. The area is heavily used, the lakes are good fishing, and for backpackers there is good camping almost anywhere.

The trailhead is at China Meadows. To get there take I-80 east of Evanston to the Fort Bridger exit, then take "I-80 Business Loop" 3 miles to a four-way intersection where you turn south to Mountain View. At Mountain View, 4.4 miles south of the four-way intersection, take Wyoming 410 west. After 5.8 more miles the paved road makes a bend west toward Robertson and the gravel road to China Meadows and Henrys Fork heads straight south. Take the road south for 11.7 miles to a junction where the road to Henrys Fork goes left and the road to China Meadows goes right. Continue another 6.7 miles past Bridger Lake and Marsh Lake to China Meadows. Continue on to the south end of the meadows, past the campground, until you come to the trailhead.

If you want to camp in this area before starting on the trail, there are campgrounds at the above lakes and at China Meadows. There are toilets, tables, grills, and a horse corral and ramp. There is no water unless you get it from the stream.

East Fork of Smiths Fork Trail (#110)

From the trailhead you start hiking up along the stream and soon reach the Wilderness boundary. It is a gentle trail most of the way. The lower part is through timber with some meadows for diversion. The east-to-west North Slope Trail crosses about 3 miles from the trailhead. About 8 miles from the trailhead you start gaining elevation and the scenic vistas start appearing.

As you enter the upper basin there is a trail junction with the trail over Bald Mountain. Continuing up, one trail goes left past East Red Castle Lake and over Smiths Fork Pass and the other branch goes right and climbs to a dead end in the upper basin.

Lower Red Castle Lake, 45 acres, lies in a beautiful alpine setting at the northern base of Red Castle Mountain. There is good camping and fishing here but the area is heavily used. A smaller lake that lies 1/2 mile east in heavy timber also has good camping and fishing.

Red Castle Lake is about 2 miles farther south, sitting against the southwest base of Red Castle Mountain and the northwest base of Wilson Peak. At 168 acres, it is the largest natural lake in the Uinta Mountains. It has many good campsites and has been stocked with cutthroat trout. It is a deep lake that is hard to fish.

Upper Red Castle Lake (26 acres) sits on a bench in a cirque at the northwestern base of Wilson Peak, about 1/2 mile south of the main lake. There is no trail to this lake but you can follow the stream up to it. It has poor campsites for backpackers and not many people try for the cutthroat trout found here.

Smiths Fork Pass (#111)

The trail to Smiths Fork Pass branches from the main trail about 1/2 mile below Lower Red Castle Lake, crosses the end of a ridge, and heads up the east drainage. It is a gradual climb all the way to the last lake.

East Red Castle Lake is about 21 acres in size and sits just off the trail below Smiths Fork Pass. There are camping spots north of the lake. Fishing is chancy but lack of heavy use should make it worth the visit.

It's about a mile and a half climb to Smiths Fork Pass at 11,800 feet. Beyond the pass it is an easy descent into Yellowstone Basin where there is a junction with the Highline Trail. Kings Peak is about 4 miles east of the pass, above the east edge of the basin.

North Slope Trail (#105)

East Fork of Smiths Fork to Lake Hessie

The North Slope Trail crosses the Smiths Fork Trail about 3 miles from the trailhead. The branch going east climbs steadily for about 2 miles to reach Lake Hessie. This lake is at the edge of the timber on a ridge continuing from the north end of Flat Top Mountain. This route to Lake Hessie is easier than the route from Henrys Fork and avoids a steep climb.

Upper Henrys Fork with Kings Peak visible through the notch in the ridge
John Veranth Photo

Henrys Fork Trailhead

Destination	Miles One Way	Elevation Gain
Elkhorn Crossing	6 1/2	900
Timberline	7	1000
Henrys Fork Lake	8	1400
Gunsight Pass	9 1/2	2500
Kings Peak - High Route	12	4200
Kings Peak - Trail Route	14 1/2	4700

USGS Maps: Gilbert Peak, Mount Powell, Kings Peak

A good trail leads into Henrys Fork Basin and is the main access from the north to Kings Peak, the highest point in Utah. The major lakes, Dollar, Henrys Fork, Grass, Blanchard, Castle and Cliff all have good fishing and camping. The lake areas, especially Dollar and Henrys Fork, are heavily used. This is a wide drainage and you can do some off-trail hiking to find many nice places to camp away from the crowds. Gunsight Pass at the head of Henrys Fork leads to the Highline Trail in the Uinta River drainage.

Henrys Fork is one of the few North Slope trailheads that can be reached in winter. The road from Lonetree is plowed to within 3 miles of the summer trailhead to give access to production oil wells in the area. Henrys Fork is a popular area for ski backpacks from mid-winter through May.

The trail begins just beyond the Henrys Fork Campground. To get there take I-80 east of Evanston to the Fort Bridger exit, then take the "I-80 Business Loop" 3 miles to a four-way intersection where you turn south to Mountain View. At Mountain View, 4.4 miles south of the four-way intersection, take Wyoming 410 west. After 5.8 more miles the paved road makes a bend west toward Robertson and the gravel road to China Meadows and Henrys Fork heads straight south.

Follow the main gravel road south from the pavement for about 12 miles to a junction where the road to China Meadows goes right and the road to Henrys Fork goes left. There are many branch roads, mostly to timber sales and drill pads, but the main road is always wider and straight ahead. Continue generally southeast for 5.3 miles from the China Meadows turnoff to a junction that is just after a series of sharp curves. The road to the Henrys Fork trailhead turns south. Straight ahead is the alternative access road that comes in 14 miles from Lonetree. Continue south for 3 more miles along Henrys Fork Creek through "The Narrows" to the trailhead. The forest road going east toward Beaver Creek and

Hole in the Rock is on the left just before the trailhead. It is about 30 miles from the four-way intersection to Henrys Fork.

Henrys Fork Trail (#117)

The trail starts at a log fence and heads up the west side of the stream. It is well traveled, both by humans and horses, and is an easy trail that climbs gradually all the way to the upper basin.

Continuing up the trail, you will reach a junction where the North Slope Trail goes east to Dead Horse Park. A mile or so farther there is a large meadow at Elkhorn Crossing. Here the North Slope Trail to Lake Hessie and Smiths Fork heads west. A loop trail that goes up the west side of Henrys Fork starts here and follows the North Slope Trail a way before turning south toward Bear, Sawmill and Grass Lakes. The main trail crosses Henrys Fork Creek here. There is a primitive footbridge a hundred yards or so downstream from the meadow.

Dollar Lake (10 acres) is the first large lake you will reach on the Henrys Fork Trail. This is heavily used so avoid it if you seek solitude. It is near timberline and mostly open country, with some sheltered campsites. It is stocked with brook and cutthroat trout.

Henrys Fork Lake (20 acres) sits mostly in the open near where the loop trail rejoins the main trail. The shoreline is heavily used for fishing so for a more secluded place to camp go up the hill a little way. This is about where the trail starts getting above timberline.

Beyond Henrys Fork Lake the trail heads along the east side of the drainage to the head of a short valley, then begins a series of switchbacks up a rocky slope to the appropriately named Gunsight Pass. It really looks like one. The trail over this pass is steep, but it is well constructed and is a good trail. At the pass you can go down the other side into the meadows and catch the Highline Trail going west to Anderson Pass or east to the Uinta River.

Henrys Fork Basin is a very popular drainage because of the many lakes, the scenery, and the access to Kings Peak. You can wander at will through open meadows in this basin. Henrys Fork has a spectacular headwall with a view of the top of Kings Peak through a notch in the ridge. Since it is near timberline it is especially important to use a camp stove and allow the limited dead wood to return to the environment.

Henrys Fork, East Fork of
Smiths Fork, East and Middle
Fork of Blacks Fork

Unfortunately, Henrys Fork accommodates a large band of sheep every summer. The sheep graze near Dollar Lake and Henrys Fork Lake rendering the place unpleasant for overnight camping. The small feeder streams may be contaminated by the livestock, so it is advisable to stay overnight at Bear Lake or Elkhorn Crossing, mentioned above. Or, if your destination is Kings Peak, Anderson Pass, or other points on the south side of the Uintas, you may proceed entirely through Henrys Basin, cross Gunsight Pass, and camp in Painter Basin at the head of the Uinta River. Good water and good camping are available in the high alpine meadow of Painter Basin below the east side of Kings Peak, and the area is easily accessible from Henrys Fork.

Branch Trails From Henrys Fork

Alligator Lake

Alligator Lake (15 acres) sits 1/2 mile off the trail about 2 miles from the campground. There is no maintained trail it, you just follow the stream up to the southwest. It is surrounded by heavy timber and has good camping but is heavily fished.

North Slope Trail (#105)

At Elkhorn Crossing the North Slope Trail heads west and follows the West Side Loop Trail for a mile then turns south. From Henrys Fork the North Slope Trail makes a steep ascent, crosses a ridge to reach Lake Hessie, then continues west into Smiths Fork.

West Side Lakes Loop

A loop trail starts at Elkhorn Crossing and goes up the west side of the Henrys Fork basin past Bear and Grass Lakes and rejoins the main trail south of Henrys Fork Lake. Off-trail hiking from this loop leads to still more lakes. You can see most of these lakes and can find them without a trail.

Bear Lake (17 acres) sits in timber country at the lower edge of the basin. It has campsites and fair fishing for cutthroat and brook trout but is heavily used. Continuing south from Bear Lake, there are several small lakes and streams. Sawmill Lake (7 acres) sits just below Bear Lake in heavy timber. There is no trail to it, you just follow the stream down from Bear Lake. It is in a secluded setting but has good campsites making it another heavy use area.

Grass Lake (5 acres) is about 3 miles south of Bear Lake, off the trail to the west. This is a shallow meadow lake which should be good fly fishing for brook and cutthroat trout. There are good camping places here.

Lake Blanchard (31 acres) is reached by a trail leading up the hill above Henrys Fork Lake but as soon as it gets to the bench above timberline it quits. This lake is in open alpine terrain at the base of Mount Powell, about a mile up the stream from Henrys Fork Lake. There is little shelter for campsites but the area is very scenic.

Cliff Lake (33 acres) is up the stream about a mile above Lake Blanchard. There is no trail. This is a deep, high lake sitting in a cirque at the southeast base of Mount Powell. Backpackers will find limited campsites and cold nights at the 11,443 foot elevation.

Kings Peak Summit (Elevation 13,528)

Follow the main trail up the east side of Henrys Fork to Gunsight Pass. From here there are two alternatives to get to Kings Peak. Both routes rejoin at Anderson Pass.

From Gunsight Pass you can continue down into the Uinta Canyon drainage and join the Highline Trail in the meadows below then take the Highline Trail back up to Anderson Pass. This route involves more elevation change but stays on maintained trails.

Most people, however, take off at Gunsight Pass and go slightly uphill then contour around to Anderson Pass. Another hiking guidebook advises against attempting this traverse but there is definitely a frequently used route leading around the hill from Gunsight Pass. The key is to look carefully from Gunsight Pass and pick out the natural route above and through the first band of cliffs. Beyond the first cliffs the terrain is less steep and you swing around the hill south and then west. You just go cross-country, gaining elevation slightly.

From Anderson Pass the peak is not difficult to climb and does not require any special equipment. It just requires strong lungs and legs and a little route finding. You do a lot of boulder hopping and ledge walking. There are sharp dropoffs to the west. The route follows the ridge crest, generally on the east, and is marked by occasional cairns.

It is about the same mileage to Kings Peak coming up from the Swift Creek Trailhead on the south, but the northern route is easier and more popular. People come from both ways, as well as up the Uinta River.

Kings Peak Summit / Thad Eagar Photo

Gilbert Peak Summit (Elevation 13,442)

Henrys Fork Trail is also a good access route to Gilbert Peak, the second highest summit in Utah. There is no trail up the peak itself. From Gunsight Pass, you can follow the ridge to the northeast to the peak, or from Dollar Lake you bushwhack and scramble up the draw to the east. It is about 3 miles to the summit from either of these two starting places. *[Reni Stott]*

Mount Powell Summit (Elevation 13,159)

This summit is on the ridge between Henrys Fork and Smiths Fork. It has multiple summits and is well north of the main Uintas crest. The ridge crest offers spectacular views of the entire range. Approach from near Henrys Fork Lake and pick out a route up the moderate-angle slopes, then hike along the ridge to the summit.

North Slope Trail (#105)

From Elkhorn Crossing to Beaver Lake there is a maintained trail marked with cairns and blazes. Since this trail is not the shortest route to any lake, it gets little use and offers a chance for solitude.

Uinta Weather

No matter how many years I spend hiking in the mountains I can never get myself to really believe how much the weather changes with elevation. I understand on a scientific level the way that temperature decreases with elevation and how clouds form as winds push over a ridge. But I never understand it on an emotional, basic instinct level until I am again high in the mountains wishing I had brought warmer clothes.

The only answer has been to faithfully stick to my equipment check list. Even if it feels silly, I shove a rain parka and sweater into my pack when it is 80 degrees and the sun is blazing overhead in town.

One weekend, while working on this book, I left for the Uintas on a warm fall day. The previous day had been hot — a record high for the date in Salt Lake. Saturday breakfast was eaten crouched down low with my back turned to a bitter wind. That afternoon, hiking above 11,000 feet, I struggled to keep the snow off my camera as I tried to capture the dark clouds swirling over the ridge. I hurried along the snow-dusted trail with my hands jammed into my pockets and wishing I had brought a wool hat and mittens. I should have known better, this happens all the time in the Uintas.

West Fork of Beaver Creek Access

Destination	Miles One Way	Elevation Gain
Wilderness Boundary	4	900
North Slope Trail Junction	5 1/2	1100
Gilbert Lake	8 1/2	1900

USGS Maps: Gilbert Peak, Hole in the Rock, Kings Peak

This trail follows the West Fork of Beaver Creek, joins the North Slope Trail, and continues on up the stream to Gilbert Lake, which sits in a basin below Gilbert Peak. Only the upper part of this drainage is in the Wilderness.

The trail begins at the end of a spur road heading south from the forest road from Henrys Fork to Hole in the Rock north of Hoop Lake. Follow the road directions for either of these trailheads to reach the end of this road. It is a rough road and can be slippery when wet. Follow the forest road for 6 miles from the Henrys Fork road or 6 miles from the Hoop Lake road past Georges Park to a point just east of Poison Mountain. Turn south on the West Fork Road. The trail begins where the road ends about 1/2 mile up the stream.

GILBERT PEAK

West Fork of Beaver Creek Trail (#119)

This is not a difficult hike as you follow the stream grade all the way. But it is a long way in through heavy timber and there are limited views until you get into the upper areas.

The main trail ends at the junction where the North Slope Trail crosses the creek. The North Slope Trail continues to Joulious Creek to the west and the Middle Fork of Beaver Creek to the east. An informal hiking trail continues on up the stream to Gilbert Lake.

Gilbert Lake (16 acres) is a fairly shallow lake sitting in mostly open country in the basin below Gilbert Peak. Not many people visit the drainages between Henrys Fork and Hoop Lake. This is a good fishing lake and not heavily used. There are two main lakes and several smaller ones in this basin. The other large one of 11 acres is just upstream about 1/2 mile from Gilbert. It is a little deeper, has some campsites and is good fishing for small brook trout and cutthroat. *[Reni Stott]*

Unnamed Lake (Number GR-154) in upper Beaver Creek Drainage
Utah Division of Wildlife Resources Photo

Georges Park Trailhead
(Middle Fork of Beaver Creek)

Destination	Miles One Way	Elevation Gain
Wilderness Boundary	1 3/4	400
North Slope Trail	4 1/2	1000
Beaver Lake	6	1300
Coffin Lake	6 3/4	1700

USGS Maps: Hole in the Rock, Fox Lake

The Wilderness boundary juts north here and parallels the road to the trailhead. From the trailhead it is a long hike through heavy timber to the upper basin where there are some open meadows. There are many small lakes all the way up, mostly to the west.

To get to the trailhead, follow the directions for Hoop Lake as far as the junction 7.4 miles from the highway. Take the right fork and go past a ranger station and some experimental beaver ponds and continue on a good gravel road for about 2 miles to the spur road to Georges Park. Head south another 2 miles to the trailhead. The parking at Georges Park is right at the trailhead. There is a sign for Middle Fork Beaver Creek Trail and North Slope Trail. There are horse unloading facilities and a fence near the parking area.

Middle Fork of Beaver Creek Trail (#120)

The trail stays east of the stream and up on the side of the mountain most of the way to avoid the many beaver ponds and boggy areas below. You will probably get your feet wet several times as all the wet places can't be avoided.

As you enter the upper basin you will join the North Slope Trail, then continue on another 2 miles to Beaver Lake. Beaver Lake (38 acres) is mostly surrounded by timber and has good camping and naturally reproducing brook trout.

Coffin Lake lies up the stream from Beaver about a mile. It's about half in the open, lying against rock slides on the west side. These upper lakes have rugged terrain and limited campsites but are in one of the least used areas of the North Slope.

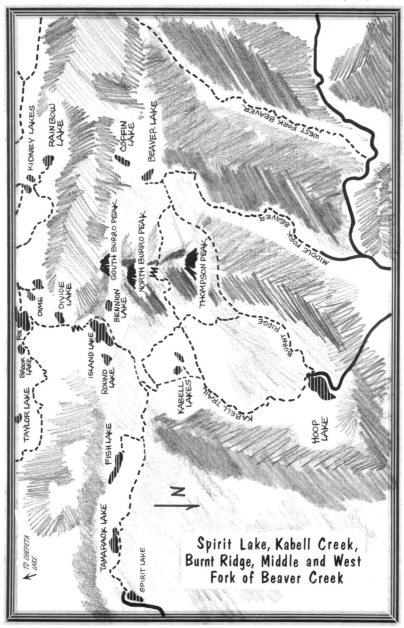

Spirit Lake, Kabell Creek, Burnt Ridge, Middle and West Fork of Beaver Creek

Hoop Lake Trailhead

Destination	Miles One Way	Elevation Gain
Wilderness Boundary	3 1/2	700
Kabell Lakes	5	1200
Island Lake	9	1600
Divide Lake Pass	11	2100
Highline Trail	12 1/2	-500 from pass

USGS Maps: Hoop Lake, Fox Lake, Hole in the Rock (Burnt Fork only)

The Hoop Lake Trailhead is a popular access to the eastern end of the Wilderness. Two main trails from here connect with the entire network of High Uinta trails. One route goes southwest, enters the Wilderness on Burnt Ridge, and continues on to the North Slope Trail and the Beaver Creek area. The other heads south to Kabell Lakes, a pair of lakes just inside the Wilderness boundary, and continues past Island Lake to an easy pass across the divide to the South Slope.

Island Lake is at the head of Burnt Fork Creek in a basin with many lakes and open meadows. This area is getting more popular because it is a mountain crossing. The trail goes above Island Lake, through the pass to Divide Lake, then down to Fox Lake in the Uinta River drainage.

To get to the trailhead, take I-80 east of Evanston, Wyoming, to the Ft. Bridger exit, then go south to Mountain View where you turn east on Wyoming 414 and continue to Lonetree. A mile east of Lonetree there is a sign on the road for "Hoop Lake-Hole in the Rock." You turn south on a good gravel road and follow the main road to a fork 7.4 miles from the highway. The right fork leads to Georges Park and the left fork goes to Hoop Lake.

Continue for another 3 1/2 miles to Hoop Lake. The road goes around the lake to the southwest side where there is a boat ramp and parking area near the concrete outlet structure. There is a separate trailhead for horse users on the southeast side of the lake.

Kabell Lake - Island Lake Trail (#122, #128, #124)

The trail to Kabell Lakes starts as an old road. You have to ford the stream. There is an easier crossing near the waterfall 30 yards downstream but expect to get your feet wet. The trail follows the lake around to its south side and then starts climbing on its way to Kabell Meadows. The trail goes mostly south from the lake, crossing Thompson Creek in about 2 miles. It then crosses over the next ridge into the Kabell Creek drainage, climbing to the meadows.

75

Kabell Lakes lie about 1/2 mile off the trail at the head of Kabell Creek in timber south of the meadows, just inside the Wilderness. There are camping places to the north and in the timber.

Continue generally south past the Kabell Lakes spur trail and cross the end of Kabell Ridge. The trail joins the North Slope Trail for a way. It's about 2 1/2 miles across this open ridge, then there is a steep switchback trail down to the upper Burnt Fork Basin. The Island Lake and the North Slope Trails separate at the top of this steep section. From here to the lakes (about 1 1/2 miles) the Island Lake Trail is rocky and boggy but is a good, well-marked trail.

Island Lake sits just at the base of the pass, near the crest of the Uinta Mountains. It is a reservoir so fluctuates in depth and acreage through the summer. It has timbered campsites around most of the lake and open areas on the side against the mountain.

Round Lake (24 acres) is a mile west of Island Lake at the base of the mountain. It has good camping spots in the pines around part of the lake. Expect good fly fishing for stocked cutthroats. Bennion Lake (8 acres) is a mile west of Island Lake at the base of North Burro Peak. There are several lakes around Bennion Lake; all have naturally reproducing cutthroat trout, and good campsites and are in a very scenic location.

Burnt Ridge Trail (#121)

The trail to Burnt Ridge turns right from the parking area and follows the stream into a muddy area where there is another trail sign. Right past this sign an obvious trail enters the trees. This trail climbs steadily and enters the Wilderness area in about 1 1/2 miles. In another mile there is a trail junction where you can go west toward Thompson Pass and Beaver Lake or east making a loop back toward Kabell Lakes.

Thompson Peak and Burro Peak

Thompson Pass crosses a wide ridge connecting Thompson Peak with North and South Burro Peaks. This is a large rounded mountain group with plenty of opportunities for above-timberline off-trail hiking to the summits in either direction.

Small lakes abound in all sorts of situation, on ridges, along mountain sides, and in piles of moraine boulders, most of them mere pools...How pure their waters are, clear as crystal in polished stone basin. — John Muir

Spirit Lake Trailhead

Destination	Miles One Way	Elevation Gain
Tamarack Lake	1 1/2	200
Wilderness Boundary	3	600
Island Lake	8 1/2	800
Fish Lake	5	-200 from pass

USGS Maps: Chepeta Lake, Fox Lake

This is another access route, along the Tamarack Trail, to Island and Round Lakes, which are within the Wilderness. The trail begins at Spirit Lake Lodge on the Middle Fork of Sheep Creek. The area south and east of Spirit Lake was not protected by the 1984 Wilderness Bill but that does not mean the area lacks wilderness values. This area is also much less crowded than the western Uintas nearer to Salt Lake City. Consider exploring some of these lakes, basins, and ridges and see for yourself.

Spirit Lake can be reached by car using either of two routes. You can start from Ft. Bridger, Wyoming, and take Wyoming 414 toward McKinnon. At a four-way junction between Burnt Fork and McKinnon, turn south onto a gravel road marked by a sign for Spirit Lake. This road passes the McKinnon Post Office. Stay on this road for approximately 10 miles until you reach a paved bridge at Hickerson Park. At this point, turn right (south) and you will reach Spirit Lake in another 8 miles.

To approach Spirit Lake from the south, take Utah 44 heading along the west side of Flaming Gorge. Then turn onto the scenic route that will later rejoin Highway 44. A forest road branches from the scenic loop and heads west past Brown and Sheep Creek Lakes. At Hickerson Park turn south just before the paved bridge and continue to Spirit Lake.

At Spirit Lake there is a Forest Service campground and south of the lake there is a large lodge that provides cabins, pack trips, and horse rentals. The main trailhead is south of the lake. Drive past the campground to where the road turns right toward the Spirit Lake Lodge. There is a small trailhead parking area and sign just before the bridge.

Tamarack Lake - Fish Lake Trail (#024 & #105)

The beginning of the trail has been reconstructed to eliminate the braided trails through the meadow. The trail crosses to the west side of the stream and heads up a short, boulder-strewn ridge, then flattens out, ascending gently to the southwest as it follows the drainage to Jessen Lake. Near pond-sized Lily Lake the trail forks. The right-hand trail goes to Tamarack Lake and beyond while the left fork goes to Jessen Lake. There are some good places to camp near the small ponds that are hidden in the trees between Jessen Lake and the ridge beyond. Tamarack Lake is 2 1/4 miles long and the best campsites are on the east side.

The main trail follows the north shore of Tamarack Lake to the west end, then climbs sharply to the Wilderness boundary on the crest of the ridge overlooking Burnt Fork. A trail branches north from here and follows the North Fork of Sheep Creek. Since the Sheep Creek Trail parallels the road to Spirit Lake it is not heavily used as a recreation access.

The main trail continues west and passes through a large alpine meadow bypassing Fish Lake, which is located against a barren ridge to the south. You have to leave the main trail to get down to Fish Lake.

Fish Lake is about 5 miles from Spirit Lake Lodge, hence it receives a moderate amount of fishing pressure from backpackers and horse riders. It is a long, narrow and deep lake. Good drinking water arises from cold springs at the east end.

After leaving the Fish Lake area, the trail proceeds westerly, passing the Burnt Fork Trail junction, then climbs through Bear Park. Here it joins the trail from the Hoop Lake Trailhead to Island Lake and to Divide Lake Pass. See the Hoop Lake Trailhead for details on this area.

The trail between Fish Lake and Island Lake has several sections that are not well maintained and may be hard to find where it crosses through wet areas.

Off-Trail Routes

From Fish Lake you can continue southwest on a faint trail around the base of the ridge to reach Burnt Fork Lake and several other small lakes that have naturally reproducing trout.

Daggett Lake Trail from Spirit Lake (#011)

The high-quality natural area on the North Slope continues far east of the Wilderness boundary. One way into this roadless area is to go east from the Spirit Lake road toward Daggett Lake. As you drive past the Spirit Lake dam there is a small parking area on the left of the road. A trail starts from here and crosses the wet meadow along the road and heads up the ridge. This trail goes through a large opening on the ridge called "Fool Hen Park" then continues through the trees along the ridge for several miles before starting down toward Daggett Lake, which is only 2 1/2 miles from the trailhead. The area has abundant campsites.

Fewer visitors go the areas farther east in the Sheep Creek Drainage, partly because the trails are in poor condition.

Deadly Lightning

Salt Lake Tribune, August 4, 1991

"A total of 11 scouts and three adult leaders from the Mormon-sponsored troop had backpacked five miles from [Hoop Lake to Kabell Meadows] ... on a three day fishing trip. A violent thunderstorm began pounding the area Friday about noon. ... four boys took refuge under a large pine tree 50 yards away from the other scouts. Electricity apparently ran down the tree and shocked the boys as they leaned against the tree." Two were killed, one was knocked unconscious but survived, and one had gotten up and was away from the tree when the lightning struck.

Dead Horse Lake — Where the Highline Trail is on the North Slope
Dave Wallace Photo

Looking West from Tungsten Pass Toward Porcupine Pass
Dave Wallace Photo

Highline Trail

Trail Section	Miles Across	Elevation Loss	Elevation Gain
Mirror Lake Highway to Rocky Sea Pass	7 1/2	-300	900
Rocky Sea Pass to Rock Creek Trail	2 1/4	-1420	
Rock Creek Trail to Dead Horse Pass	5 1/2		1800
Dead Horse Pass to Dead Horse Lake	1	-720	
Dead Horse Lake to Red Knob Pass	2 1/2		1120
Red Knob Pass to Lake Fork Trail	3 1/2	-1600	
Lake Fork Trail to Porcupine Pass	8 1/2		1840
Porcupine Pass to Tungsten Pass	2 1/2	-900	100
Tungsten Pass to Anderson Pass	6 3/4	-400	1300
Anderson Pass to Painter Basin	3	-1500	
Painter Basin to Fox Lake	10 1/2	-600	1000
Fox Lake to North Pole Pass	2 1/2		1500
North Pole Pass to Chepeta Lake Road	5 3/4	-1600	
Chepeta Lake to Whiterocks Divide	14	-200	1000
Whiterocks Divide to Leidy Peak Trailhead	7 1/2	-1200	1000

Note: Only the major elevation changes between passes and stream crossings or trail junctions are indicated. The minor up and down sections on long, generally level trail sections are not included.

The Highline Trail across the Uintas is one of the great Wilderness trails of the West. From the trailhead on the Mirror Lake Highway to the next road access is over 60 miles of Wilderness hiking, mostly near or above timberline.

It crosses the heads of the major drainages along the backbone of the Uintas, staying between 10,000 and 12,600 foot elevation most of the way. Except for the short section at Dead Horse Lake, the trail stays south of the divide. The individual trailhead descriptions in this book list the miles and elevation gain from the road to the Highline Trail along each drainage. The Highline Trail itself is described in detail as part of the trail system in each drainage.

There are many ways to enjoy the Highline Trail. There is nothing like an end-to-end hike to experience the magnificent alpine terrain of the High Uintas but it requires a long car shuttle. Most visitors have to be content with a loop hike going up one drainage, traveling along part of the Highline Trail and returning to their car by another trail. On a three-day backpack it is possible to explore a section of the Highline Trail by doing a day hike from a base camp high on the main trail coming up one of the drainages.

Descending from Rocky Sea Pass into Upper Rock Creek / John Veranth Photo

THE SOUTH SLOPE

Introduction

The South Slope has wide, branching drainages with extensive basins and flat areas high above the streams. Intermediate ridges within the basins and even the divides between the major drainages are crossed by maintained trails and by cross-country routes making loop hikes feasible and popular.

The Naturalist Basin, Grandaddy Lakes Basin and Brown Duck Basin are the most heavily used areas on the South Slope. Rock Creek, Lake Fork, and Uinta Canyon have long sections where the trail climbs slowly through dense timber for many miles before approaching timberline and open country. Many backpackers prefer to reach the upper basins of the South Slope drainages from the Highline Trail or by crossing from the North Slope.

Mirror Lake Highway

The Mirror Lake Highway is an excellent paved road that starts in Kamas as Utah Highway 150, follows the Provo River to Bald Mountain Pass at 10,620 feet, dips down into the Duchesne River drainage as it goes past Mirror Lake, then crosses Hayden Pass (10,347 feet) near the Highline Trailhead and continues down into the Bear River drainage. Farther north it leaves the National Forest, enters Wyoming and ends at Evanston. It is groomed for snowmobiles in the winter. This 80-mile-long highway was completed in 1960 and this increased recreational use in the area.

The scenic overlook 30 miles from Kamas gives the opportunity for anyone to see far into the Wilderness area and to sense its scale and grandeur. Forest Service campgrounds along the highway fill up fast on summer weekends and nearby backcountry trails and lakes are also busy.

The most heavily used section of the High Uintas Wilderness is the western end, near the Mirror Lake Highway. The Mirror Lake and Highline Trailheads are along the highway and the Duchesne River Access and the Christmas Meadows Trailhead are reached by spur roads.

This guidebook covers the High Uintas Wilderness east of the Mirror Lake Highway, but there is good hiking in the Mount Watson roadless area on the west side of the road too.

Highline Trailhead

Destination	Miles One Way	Elevation Gain
Wilderness Boundary	3/4	-200
Naturalist Basin	6	800
Four Lakes Basin	7 3/4	700
Rocky Sea Pass	7 1/2	1200
Governor Dern Lake	8 1/2	300

USGS Maps: Hayden Peak

This popular trailhead is near the Wilderness boundary and a short drive on paved highways from the Wasatch Front. It is near the divide between the Bear River and the Duchesne River and offers the best access route to Wilder Lake, Naturalist Basin, Pinto Lake, Four Lakes Basin and Rocky Sea Pass. These nearby places offer a sampling of the scenic beauties to be found throughout the High Uintas but they are crowded on popular weekends.

This trailhead is along the Mirror Lake Highway, 34 miles northeast of Kamas and 44 miles south of Evanston. It is about 3 miles north of Mirror Lake, just north of the Butterfly Lake Campground. It is a modern trailhead with parking, horse unloading, picnic area and toilets. No camping is allowed right at the trailhead but there are several developed campgrounds nearby.

Highline Trail (#083) - Highway to Rocky Sea Pass

The well-marked and heavily-used trail begins beyond the signboard. The Highline Trail starts here and is described in sections as it crosses each major drainage. You go slightly downhill as you enter the upper basin of the Duchesne River. In about 1/2 mile, the connecting trail coming up from Mirror Lake joins from the right and the main trail toward Rocky Sea Pass is to the left. A short way farther is the Wilderness boundary sign and a registration box.

The trail descends gradually until you reach Scudder Lake. A short distance past the junction with the Mirror Lake Trail, you can see Scudder Lake through the trees to the south. It is a small lake surrounded by timber and has some nice campsites.

Proceeding east on the trail from Scudder Lake, there are some ups and downs but it's mostly pretty level for the next 3 miles until you get to the base of Rocky Sea Pass. You're in timber country from the beginning and remain so all the way to Rocky Sea Pass.

Past Scudder Lake and about 2 1/2 miles from the trailhead, you come to a trail going off to the south to Wilder, Wyman, and Packard Lakes. About 1 1/2 miles past the Wilder Lake turnoff and about 4 miles from the Highline Trailhead, is the Naturalist Basin trail junction. Since so many people go to Naturalist Basin the branch looks like the main trail. Be sure to take the right fork if you are continuing on the Highline Trail.

About a mile from the Naturalist Basin Trail is a junction with a trail going south. This trail splits with one branch going southwest down the East Fork of the Duchesne River and the other leading southeast toward Pinto Lakes and Grandaddy Lake Basin.

The next main junction on the Highline Trail after passing the East Fork - Pinto Lake Trail is near Pigeon Milk Spring. Near the springs, to the south and off the trail, lie lakes Carolyn and Olga. These are very pretty mountain lakes sitting in partly timbered country. Both have nice camping areas. Arctic grayling may be caught in Carolyn Lake but there are no fish in Olga Lake.

From the junction near the springs, you can go east on the Highline Trail to Rocky Sea Pass and into the head of Rock Creek Basin. Or you can go south to Four Lakes Basin or Grandaddy Basin and you can continue south to the Grandview Trailhead.

Pigeon Milk Spring is a large flow gushing out from under the boulder-covered hillside. It is so named because of its milky color caused by "glacial flour." Ancient glaciers grinding huge rocks together formed a very fine powder which is still leaching out.

The Highline Trail continues east from near Pigeon Milk Spring and starts to climb towards Rocky Sea Pass. It is a steep, rough, and rocky trail, but well worth the effort. The trails in the area are well marked with tree blazes or with rock cairns above the timberline. The pass is above timberline and is on a big open bald ridge, entirely covered with boulders — like a huge rocky sea.

From the pass, you get a tremendous view back over the Duchesne drainage, and looking ahead you have a breath-taking panoramic view of the upper Rock Creek drainage. This country is huge, and at the pass this realization overwhelms you. Rocky Sea Pass is a popular backpack access to upper Rock Creek. Coming from Mirror Lake is shorter and more scenic than the hike up Rock Creek. See the Rock Creek description for the continuation of the Highline Trail.

Spur Trails from the Highline Trail

Wilder and Packard Lake Trail (#059)

Down this short but fairly steep trail are three lakes: Wilder, Wyman, and Packard. These lakes are surrounded by timber and have good campsites. You may find a crowd at Wilder, but if you go on to Packard, another 3/4 mile, you usually will find fewer campers there. All three lakes are stocked with brook trout.

Naturalist Basin Trail (#084)

Naturalist Basin is a large area, very pretty, with a very popular group of lakes scattered among the meadows and mixed pine and spruce-fir forest near timberline. The basin is surrounded on three sides by scenic mountains and and is at the base of Mount Agassiz. This is a favorite area for scouts; so if you're seeking seclusion, try another basin. The crowds seem to congregate at the first meadow junction, and at Jordan and Morat lakes. Many campsites in Naturalist Basin are too close to the water and are causing environmental damage. Heavy use has stripped the basin clear of firewood. Pick your site carefully.

This trail climbs about 400 feet from the Highline junction before leveling out in the basin. About a mile into the basin, there is a trail junction in a meadow. The left fork here takes you to Blue and Morat Lakes which lie a mile away, up in a high basin in a very scenic and pretty area. These lakes are usually frozen over until the middle of July. Fly fishing is usually good for brook trout, rainbow, and cutthroat trout.

On past the first junction in Naturalist Basin about 1/2 mile, you will reach Jordan Lake. This is quite a large lake, with timber around part of it, and with very heavy camping use. Fishing pressure is heavy for small brook trout, so if you are on a fishing trip only, this is not the best. Evermann Lake lies to the southeast of Jordan and is good for camping but has no fish in it.

Going on past Jordan Lake, you will climb up onto a bench where you will find Shaler, Faxon, and LeConte Lakes in the upper basin. These are high alpine lakes sitting in rocky, open country with poor campsites. Shaler is good for fly fishing for cutthroat but Faxon is shallow so it winter kills and has no fish.

South to Pinto and Grandaddy Lakes (#089)

A trail branches from the Highline Trail 5 miles from the trailhead and starts down the East Fork of the Duchesne River.

About 1 1/2 miles down this trail, a branch to the south leads over to Pinto Lake and on to a large group of lakes — Rainbow, Pine Island, Palisade and many more in Grandaddy Basin south of Governor Dern Lake. See the Grandview Trailhead description for details about trails in this area.

This route is the best way to get to Grandaddy Basin if you are starting from the Mirror Lake Highway. If you go down the Duchesne River, you have a hard climb back up the East Fork to get to this same area. If you start from the Highline Trailhead, you have a fairly level trail all the way into Grandaddy Basin.

Four Lakes Basin Trail (#085, #102)

From the junction near Pigeon Milk Spring a trail goes south to Four Lakes Basin. It crosses the end of a boulder-covered ridge and about 1 1/2 miles south and east of Pigeon Milk Spring reaches a nice viewpoint overlooking Four Lakes Basin. This basin, about 8 miles from the trailhead, is a very scenic, open area at the base of glaciated mountains. It consists of four good fishing lakes, Jean, Dean, Dale, and Daynes. These lakes, being farther in, don't get nearly as heavy use as Naturalist Basin. Cutthroat, brook trout and grayling are found here. In addition to the official trails, a large number of informal trails and off-trail cross-country routes exist in this area. See Grandaddy Basin Trailhead for more information on this area.

Four Lakes Basin to Rainbow Lake (#083, #074)

A trail goes from Daynes Lake southwest for 2 miles through timber to connect with the Grandaddy Basin trail network near Rainbow Lake. This trail can be used to make a backpacking loop between the lake basins and back to the Highline Trail.

Hayden Peak Summit (Elevation 12,497)

This rugged peak on the ridge between the Mirror Lake Highway and the McPheters Lake area is a popular summit destination. Despite the cliffs and pinnacles, no technical climbing is involved, but route finding and scrambling can be challenging.

Park at the trailhead and look east. There is a slide area to the south of the peak and a spur ridge going toward you. These are your landmarks. Bushwhack to the base of the ridge. One route is to go up the spur ridge climbing from the tip and continuing to the main ridge. You climb steadily through the trees. An equally good alternative is to ascend the rock slide to the ridge. As you get to the top there is a small cliff that you need to scramble through. Either way you end up on the ridge connecting Hayden and Mount Agassiz which is to the southeast.

Continue north along the ridge to Hayden. The last little bit near the Hayden summit goes above cliffs and around pinnacles. Careful route finding plus some basic rock climbing skill is recommended. If the route suddenly seems dangerously difficult, back off and look around for a better variation until you find your way to the top. *[Duke Moscon]*

Mount Agassiz Summit (Elevation 12,428)

This peak can be climbed from the Highline Trailhead, from the Ryder Lake area, or from Blue Lake in Naturalist Basin. The route from the Mirror Lake Highway starts the same as for Hayden Peak. From the crest of the ridge connecting the two summits you turn southeast and hike along an open, rounded ridge crest all the way to Mount Agassiz.

Up and Over to Stillwater Fork (Off-Trail)

On the ridge just south of Hayden Peak one can look down on McPheters Lake. Hikers go over the ridge to get to the lake but the descent on the other side involves hopping over giant boulders and there are some hidden cliffs.

Finding the right pass is the key to avoiding the cliffs on the east side. Do not take the pass close to Mount Agassiz that looks like the low spot on the ridge. Take the definite notch that is almost straight west from the Highline Trailhead. This route is passable for strong day hikers but is tricky for backpackers. *[Jon Eagar]*

— The year that this updated book was finished, the Forest Service seriously analyzed including the area between the Mirror Lake campground and the Highline Trail as part of the Murdock Mountain timber sale. This timber havest alternative was rejected, for now. The Forest Service is under incredible pressure from timber interests to "get out the cut." Social value judgments determine forest priorities. Citizens must make their views known if the scenic and recreational values of standing forests and the ecological values of standing dead snags and decaying logs are to be recognized. —

Mirror Lake Trailhead

Destination	Miles One Way	Elevation Gain
Highline Trail Junction	1 3/4	200
East Fork of Duchesne Trail	3 1/2	-1200

USGS Maps: Mirror Lake*, Hayden Peak

This trailhead is the beginning of two trails, one going down the Duchesne River along the west edge of the Wilderness and the other connecting with the Highline Trail going east.

This trailhead is located at the end of a spur road from the Mirror Lake Campground. Just a short distance beyond, there is a large parking lot with mangers and unloading facilities for horses. To reach it, take the Mirror Lake to the turnoff 31 miles east of Kamas or 47 miles south of Evanston. Signs indicate the campground (fee area) and trailhead parking area. There are a registration box and a sign indicating the trailhead. There are a number of minor, unofficial trails around the campground. A second trailhead for the Mirror Lake Trail is at the north end of the campground but these trails join in 1/4 mile.

Mirror Lake Trail (Connection to Highline Trail)

The trail north from Mirror Lake swings around to the left and climbs slightly to join the Highline Trail in about 1 3/4 miles. It begins by paralleling the main campground, then swings off to the east to reach Bonnie Lake in about 1/2 mile.

Bonnie Lake is about 4 acres in size, and is a shallow lake sitting in an open meadow. It is outside the Wilderness and is visited quite heavily. Southeast of Bonnie about 1/2 mile is Blythe Lake, about half the size of Bonnie. There is no trail connecting these two but being near Mirror Lake, Blythe also gets heavy usage. These lakes are stocked frequently with brook trout, but get intense fishing pressure since they are close to the highway.

From Bonnie, the trail continues gradually climbing through the timber to the east and joins the Highline Trail in about a mile. See the Highline Trail description for the continuation of the combined trail.

Duchesne River Trail - South from Mirror Lake

The trail down the North Fork of the Duchesne goes 3 1/2 miles to the junction with the trail up the East Fork which climbs back to the Pinto Lakes area. The Duchesne River Trail continues to the Duchesne Tunnel entrance (7 miles) and then another 5 miles to end at a road coming up the river from near the Iron Mine Campground. Although the trail runs right along the Wilderness boundary it is not an easy access into the Wilderness because the Duchesne River canyon sides are steep. There is no bridge across the Duchesne River and the ford can be difficult in spring. The East Fork Trail connects with the Highline Trail and the Pinto Lakes area trails but from Mirror Lake you drop down to the river and have to climb back up the East Fork again. See the Duchesne River Access description for this section. *[Duke Moscon]*

Mount Agassiz from the Highline Trail / John Veranth Photo

Duchesne River Access

Destination	Miles One Way	Elevation Gain
East Fork Trail Junction	3 1/2	600
Mill Flat Trailhead	5	-500
Highline Trail Junction	7	1980
Governor Dern Lake	7 3/4	1800

USGS Maps: Mirror Lake, Iron Mine Mountain, Hayden Peak

The road to the East Portal of the Duchesne Tunnel is a worthwhile access point if you have a high-clearance vehicle. The Duchesne River offers pleasant river-side hiking but has limited access into the Wilderness. The north end of the Duchesne River Trail is reached from Mirror Lake and the south end is at Mill Flat. Both are readily accessible by passenger car.

To get to the east portal of the Duchesne Tunnel Trailhead, you take the road signed "Murdock Basin Road" which is about 22 miles from the start of the Mirror Lake Highway in Kamas. The road is paved at the start, crosses a bridge and changes to gravel and continues as a maintained gravel road for 2 miles to where the Murdock Basin Road turns left. The right fork is a rougher road that begins to descend toward the Duchesne River. After another 2.5 miles there is a series of narrow hairpin turns. The road to the trailhead branches left from the center of the second hairpin turn and fades out near the trailhead sign, where there is room to park. If you continue around the hairpin turn the road splits and the left branch goes 0.2 mile down to the tunnel portal at the river.

Mill Flat Trailhead

The Duchesne River Trail follows the west edge of the Wilderness Area from Mill Flat on the south, past the road to the East Portal of the Duchesne Tunnel and on to Mirror Lake.

To get to the Mill Flat Trailhead follow the road directions for the Grandview Trailhead from Hanna to Defa's Dude Ranch. Instead of taking the turnoff up Hades Canyon stay along the river for another 2 miles to the end. The road is well maintained as far as the Iron Mine Campground then gets rougher, fords a small stream, and ends at a large undeveloped flat area about 1/2 mile beyond the campground.

Duchesne River Trail (#980) - North from Mill Flat

The Duchesne River Trial is a stream-side trail along the bottom of a scenic V-notch canyon. It is more important as a route for its own sake than as an access to the Wilderness. Entering the Wilderness from this trail anywhere south of the East Fork Trail to Pinto Lakes involves a steep off-trail climb up the sidewall of the Duchesne River canyon.

The south section of the trail starts on the east side of the river then fords to the west. It is 5 miles between the trailhead at Mill Flat and the Duchesne Tunnel access at the end of the road coming from Hanna. This is a pleasant route for hikers, horse riders, and anglers who want to stay near a stream and avoid elevation gain. The trail is outside the wilderness and is currently open to vehicles but it passes through soft wet areas.

The north section of the trail between Mirror Lake and the Duchesne Tunnel access receives little use and is not maintained on a regular basis. It goes up the river on its west bank then branches. The west fork continues up the river and ends at the Mirror Lake Campground and the east branch goes to Pinto Lakes.

East Fork of Duchesne River Trail (#087, #088)

The trail crosses the river, enters the Wilderness, and proceeds up the East Fork of the Duchesne River. This trail receives considerable horse use. The trail climbs about 800 feet in about 2 1/2 miles to the junction where a branch trail takes off to the right and climbs to the Pinto-Governor Dern Lakes area. This trail, the Skinner Cutoff Trail, climbs steeply for about 1/2 mile then levels off as you approach Pinto Lake, which is about 1 1/2 miles from the trail junction. See Grandaddy Basin, listed under the Grandview Trailhead, for these lake descriptions.

Staying on the East Fork Trail, you will pass another trail, Pinto Lake-East Fork Trail, in about 1 mile, leading off to the right going back to Pinto Lake, about 1 1/2 miles away. Continuing farther up the East Fork, you reach the Highline Trail in about 2 miles. At the Highline Trail junction you will be 1 1/2 miles from the Naturalist Basin turnoff and 7 miles from the Mirror Lake Trailhead. Turning to the right on the Highline Trail leads to Rocky Sea Pass, the gateway to the entire Wilderness lying to the east. [Duke Moscon]

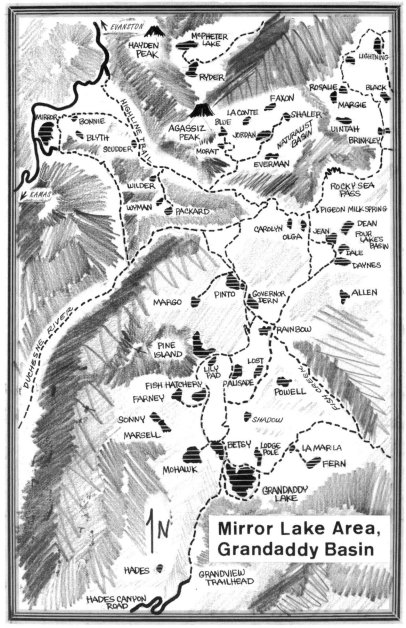

Mirror Lake Area, Grandaddy Basin

Grandview Trailhead

Destination	Miles One Way	Elevation Gain
Hades Pass	2 1/4	940
Grandaddy Lake	3	-300 from pass
Rainbow Lake	6 1/2	-600 from pass
Four Lakes Basin	8 1/2	1640
Highline Trail Junction	9	1500
Rocky Sea Pass	10	2200
Rock Creek Trail via LaMarla	12 1/2	-2600 from pass

USGS Maps: Grandaddy Lake, Hayden Peak

Grandaddy Basin is second only to Naturalist Basin in popularity. The trailhead is at about 10,000 feet, the Wilderness Boundary is just beyond the end of the road, and Grandaddy Lake is less than 2 hours away. This trailhead offers fast, easy access to a beautiful basin with many lakes and streams in gently sloping terrain. This is high country and the forest is broken by frequent clearings and meadows offering views of the surrounding peaks. Grandaddy Basin is in the Rock Creek drainage, but just north of Pinto Lake the runoff switches to the East Fork of the Duchesne River. There is no distinct ridge separating the two watersheds so the hiking is fairly level throughout the area.

The south entrance to Grandaddy Basin is from the Grandview Trailhead near the top of Hades Canyon far above the Duchesne River. Camping is available at three Forest Service campgrounds along the Duchesne River. Horses and guides may be obtained at Defa's Dude Ranch, on the Duchesne River.

There are several ways to reach this trailhead, depending on whether you're coming from Duchesne, the Wasatch Front, or the Mirror Lake area, but they all join 2.2 miles north of the Hanna post office at the intersection of Utah 35 and the forest road which goes up the North Fork of the Duchesne River.

The direct route is to take US 40 to the junction with Utah 208 about 5 miles east of Fruitland and 17 miles west of Duchesne. Take Utah 208 north for 10 miles to the junction with Utah 35 and head west for another 11 miles through Tabiona and Hanna, to the Stockmore Guard Station at the junction of Utah 35 and Forest Road 144 up the North Fork of the Duchesne River. The pavement ends here and the road north is well maintained gravel.

From Francis via Utah 35: A shorter route from the Wasatch Front is to take Utah 35 from Francis, through Woodland, and over Wolf Creek Summit to the junction north of Hanna. This state highway is currently a gravel road for 21 miles. There are plans to pave this road but for now you will be doing well to average 25 mph on the gravel section. Take US 189 to the junction with Utah 35 in Francis, 2 miles south of Kamas, and go east on Utah 35. It is 33 miles from here to the junction with the road up the north fork of the Duchesne. This is a scenic road across a forested ridge, past a good campground at Wolf Creek summit, and down along the West Fork of the Duchesne River to the junction with Forest Road No. 144. The scenic drive through the Uinta National Forest offsets the bumpy ride. A forest road connects Utah 35 with the Mirror Lake Highway near Soapstone.

From the junction 2.2 miles north of Hanna the route turns up the North Fork of the Duchesne River and follows a well maintained gravel road for 6.7 miles to the Hades Canyon turnoff, just past Defa's Dude Ranch.

The 6-mile road from the Hades Canyon turnoff to the Grandview Trailhead is a maintained single-lane gravel road with turnouts for passing. There are some exposed rocks and there are steep dropoffs on the side. It is not a road for persons who are afraid of dropoffs nor for motor homes pulling a trailer or other oversized vehicles. But it is definitely suitable for passenger cars.

Grandview is a nice, recently-constructed trailhead with concrete toilet facilities, horse trailer parking, backpacker parking, and several picnic tables. Also, there is a Forest Service registry box; everyone taking the trail should register.

Hades Pass to Rocky Sea Pass Trail (#074)

The trail is well maintained and rises with gentle switchbacks for the first 1/4 mile then continues to rise gently as you hike through the forest to the pass. From the pass, at 11,000 feet elevation, there are excellent views of the Grandaddy Lake area and far beyond over the entire timber-covered basin, with its many lakes and meadows.

Grandaddy Lake is a large lake, about 170 acres, surrounded by lodgepole pines and Engleman spruce. There is plenty of camping space but it is heavily used. The southwest side is the best, as the other side is boggy. Fishing is fair for cutthroat and brook trout. A 2 1/2 mile loop route goes around the lake. This is mostly used by anglers and is boggy on the southeast side of the lake.

From Grandaddy Lake you can take the LaMarla Lake Trail going east down to Rock Creek (see LaMarla Lake Trail description) or continue north on the Hades Trail.

Betsy Lake is next on the Hades Trail, about 1/4 mile from Grandaddy. It's much the same as Grandaddy except it's smaller (about 30 acres), with camping on all sides. Mohawk Lake is only 1/2 mile from Betsy over fairly level ground. It's rather large, 50 acres, with good campsites and some springs on the south side. This is a little way off the beaten track so it is less heavily used.

The Pine Island Loop Trail branches to the west at Betsy Lake and the Hades Trail continues another mile to Brinton Meadow where the Palisade Lake Trail branches to the left. Shadow Lake is a small lake (7 acres) containing naturally reproducing brook and cutthroat trout. There is an unmaintained trail leading to it. The turnoff is located on the Hades Trail, about 400 feet east of the Palisade Trail junction. You can see the lake from the trail; just hike off the hill over to it.

The Hades to Rocky Sea Pass Trail continues for another 2 miles to Rainbow Lake where there are two major trail junctions. The Fish Creek Trail goes southeast down into the Rock Creek drainage. A short distance farther the trail to Governors and Pinto branches off to the northwest. The trail going northwest can be considered an extension of the Fish Creek Trail or the north end of the Pine Island Loop. The Hades Trail continues northeast to Four Lakes Basin and Rocky Sea Pass. This maze of trails provides a lot of opportunity for day hikes from a base camp anywhere in the area.

Continuing on the Hades Trail, you are in timber for another mile and climb gradually all the way on a good trail until you reach Bedground Lake. At Bedground Lake, the trail forks again. There is a side trail that goes 1 mile east into Four Lakes Basin, then turns back northwest to rejoin the main trail. The direct trail goes 1 1/2 miles north to the junction with the Highline Trail. The combined trails then continue another 1 1/2 miles to Rocky Sea Pass.

Side Trails from the Hades Trail

East Grandaddy Mountain Summit

The mountain just to the east of the pass above Grandaddy Lake can be reached by fairly straightforward off-trail boulder-hopping up the slope. This is a flat-topped plateau with the Wilderness boundary going down the middle and offers excellent views. You can continue along the ridge for 4 miles to the far end overlooking Rock Creek.

LaMarla Lake -West Fork of Rock Creek Trail (#073)

From the east side of Grandaddy Lake, there is a trail that goes down to Lodgepole Lake and on past LaMarla Lake and ties into the West Fork of Rock Creek, a total of 3 miles. The first part of the trail, after leaving Grandaddy Lake, includes about 1/4 mile that switchbacks straight down. Lodgepole Lake sits several hundred feet lower than Grandaddy. This is a steep, narrow trail and can be a little hairy for horses but should be no problem for hikers. Lodgepole is medium sized (20 acres), a nice place to camp, and has been stocked with Eastern brook trout.

LaMarla Lake is a mile past Lodgepole Lake on the trail. It is quite small (3 acres) and contains no fish. The LaMarla Trail continues on and meets the Fish Creek Trail. The combined trails drop steadily down the West Fork and join the Rock Creek Trail not far from the Upper Stillwater Reservoir.

Fern Lake lies off the trail about 3/4 mile southeast of LaMarla Lake. Fern is a good fishing lake and actually doesn't get much use. This would be a good place to get away from it all. Some campers at Grandaddy will hike over to Fern for the day, it's about 2 miles between the lakes.

Grandaddy Basin From Hades Pass
John Veranth Photo

Docs Lake and Red Cliffs Lake lie about a mile and a half off the LaMarla-West Fork Trail. There is no trail and no sign indicating where to leave the trail, only a beaten path leading up to the lakes. Docs Lake is about 15 acres, fairly deep, and contains trout. Red Cliff, to the west of Docs, is small and shallow and probably has no fish. There are camping places at both lakes for backpackers.

Pine Island Loop Trail (#079)

The best bet for exploring Grandaddy Basin is to take this 9-mile loop. Starting from Betsy Lake it goes to Fish Hatchery Lake, Pine Island, Governor, and around to Rainbow where it rejoins the main Hades to Rocky Sea Pass Trail which can be followed back south past Lost Lake, across Brinton Meadows, and back to Betsy.

Fish Hatchery Lake is about a mile from Betsy on the loop trail. It's a little smaller than Betsy and has good camping in heavy timber but is heavily fished for brook trout.

Farney Lake is about 1/2 mile from Fish Hatchery, off the loop trail to the west. The unmaintained trail to this lake is only a beaten path. Farney is a very pretty lake with good camping but has no fish; it winter kills. Sonny and Marsell Lakes have no trail but may be reached from Farney. They're about 1/2 directly south through the timber. You can't see them from Farney, but they are no trouble to find. These lakes are in the Duchesne River drainage so going downstream is away from Grandaddy Basin.

Pine Island Lake is next on the loop trail after leaving Fish Hatchery. It is one of the larger lakes (80 acres), located at the base of a steep talus slope. Lily Pad Lake is across the trail from Pine Island Lake. It's a small lake with lily pads covering its surface. These will start blooming in mid-July some years, and will continue about a month. It has a rocky shore but there is good camping.

Fish Creek is reached in 2 miles from Pine Island. About 1/2 mile before the junction are some switchbacks. It's fairly steep coming back up, but going in this direction is no problem. Right at the bottom a shortcut trail to Governors Lake takes off to the left. The main trail along Fish Creek is a short distance farther ahead. At this trail junction, near Governors Lake, you are half way between the Grandview and Mirror Lake Trailheads, 9 miles each way.

Rainbow Lake is 1 mile farther on the loop trail. It is a small lake (18 acres) and the lowest in the Grandaddy Basin. Camping is good here. Brook trout and cutthroat are occasionally stocked. Here the Pine Island Loop rejoins the main Hades to Rocky Sea Pass Trail.

Lost Lake is 1 mile south of Rainbow on the return part of the Pine Island Loop Trail. Flat places alternate with rolling climbs from here back to the start of the loop at Betsy Lake.

Powell Lake is 1/2 mile southeast of Lost Lake. There is a trail between the two, maintained but in poor condition. Brinton Meadows is a mile from Lost Lake, returning on the loop trail, and 2 miles north of Betsy Lake on the Hades Trail.

Palisade Lake Trail (#080)

This takes off from the Hades Trail north of Brinton Meadows and connects with the Pine Island Loop just east of Pine Island Lake. It's easy to follow but rocky and in poor condition. Many people use it, though. Palisade Lake is about 3 miles from Betsy. The large ledge on the west of the lake, about 50 feet above the water, is one of the prettiest places in the basin. There is good camping near Palisade Lake and at Brinton Meadows.

Fish Creek Trail — East to Rock Creek (#076)

From Rainbow Lake, you can go down Fish Creek to Rock Creek (7 miles) then on down about 2 miles to the trailhead at Upper Stillwater Reservoir. Fish Creek joins the West Fork of Rock Creek trail coming from LaMarla Lake.

Fish Creek Trail — West to Skinner Cutoff Trail (#076)

From the junction on the Hades Trail north of Rainbow Lake a continuation of the Fish Creek Trail heads northwest. This trail goes to Pinto Lake and the next 1/2 mile is also part of the Pine Island Lake Loop. This trail continues past Governor Dern and Pinto Lakes to the junction where the Skinner Cutoff goes northwest to the East Fork of the Duchesne and the other trail goes northeast to join the Highline Trail.

Governor Dern Lake (also called Governors Lake) is a 22 acre, shallow lake that lies along the Fish Creek Trail 1 mile northwest of Rainbow Lake and just southeast of Pinto Lake. The lake has plenty of good campsites.

Pinto Lake is a popular fishing lake, about 47 acres, with good fishing and camping. It lies at the upper end of the Fish Creek Trail, 2 miles above Rainbow Lake.

Margo Lake Trail

There is an unmaintained trail leading from the northern side of Pinto Lake to Margo Lake. Margo is a medium-sized lake, with camping in the meadow on the east side. It is a steep hike, gaining about 500 feet.

From Margo, you can either return on the trail from Pinto Lake or cross over to Pine Island Lake and get back on the trail there. To do this off-trail route go up the drainage on the southwest end of the lake — it's a gentle climb to the saddle — then veer off to the southeast to come down to the northeast side of Pine Island. Backpackers would have no problem handling this. Take care going up from Margo that you go only south to the divide. If you went west or southwest, you could cross over into the Duchesne River drainage and be in trouble. From Pine Island you can go south along the east side and hit the trail which crosses the south end of the lake between it and Lily Lake.

Four Lakes Basin Area (#083)

From Bedground Lake, a side trail passes through Four Lakes Basin. This basin consists of four lakes sitting in scattered pockets of timber against the base of the mountains. There are plenty of good campsites throughout the basin. You are right near timberline here and there is a lot of variety: forest, meadows, swampy areas, and open rocky slopes. This is a scenic basin with lots of places to wander on day hikes.

The trail passes Daynes, Dale and Jean Lakes. Dean Lake sits directly behind Jean, along the base of the mountain. These are beautiful glacial lakes, from 15 to 25 acres in size. Grayling may be taken here, in addition to cutthroat and brook trout. Allen Lake is 1 mile south of Daynes Lake and is reached by a trail which takes off between Daynes and Bedground Lakes. Allen is about 15 acres in size, bordered by timber on one side and a meadow on the other.

The Four Lakes Basin is probably more often reached from Mirror Lake than from Grandview. It is closer this way, being 9 miles along the Highline Trail, turning off at Pigeon Milk Spring.

An unmaintained trail goes east between Daynes and Dale Lakes and climbs to Cyclone Pass on the rim of the basin. From the pass, you can boulder hop 1/4 mile north to Thompson Lake. There is good fishing here. Few visit it and horses can't get there. Camping is limited to a few rocky sites at the north end.

From Cyclone Pass, you can also hike cross-country over to Sea Lion Lake. This again is not a horse trail. From Sea Lion it's also possible to come down the ridge and get to Slide and Frances Lakes. From all these lakes east of Cyclone Pass it is dangerous and very difficult to try to hike down to Rock Creek because of cliffs. It is advisable to return to Four Lakes Basin.

Pinto Lake - Four Lakes Loop (#074, #076, #083, #089)

A good hiking, camping and fishing loop can be made by going from Four Lakes Basin to Rainbow, Governors, Pinto, Skinners Cutoff, Carolyn, Olga and back to Four Lakes Basin. This loop can be started at any point with access being from the Highline Trail, Fish Creek Trail, Hades - Rocky Sea Pass Trail, or Duchesne East Fork Trail. The entire area is approximately the same elevation, and is covered with timber and open meadows, interspersed with many smaller lakes.

Arta Lake Road

Arta Lake is near the head of the South Fork of Rock Creek, a minor drainage running between Grandaddy Mountain and the Stillwater Dam. This drainage offers opportunity for day hiking and car camping outside the Wilderness boundary. One unmaintained trail and several difficult off-trail routes lead into the Wilderness from this drainage.

A gravel road heads west from the entrance to the Rock Creek Trailhead and goes over a scenic pass to Hanna. The Arta Lake Road branches north 1.9 miles east of the start of this gravel road and continues for 4.6 miles to a turnaround near the end of the drainage. The road is rough and not well maintained but passenger cars can make it.

High Route above Stillwater Reservoir (#141)

There is a large parking area on the north side of the Arta Lake Road 1.4 miles from the junction with the road to Hanna. A trail starts from here and goes high on the ridge overlooking Upper Stillwater Reservoir then drops down and enters the Wilderness just before joining the West Fork Trail. This trail was built to modern Forest Service standards to detour backcountry users around the dam construction site and has been semi-abandoned since the heavy construction was completed.

It is a steep trail for the Uintas. It climbs 1000 feet to the ridge and then drops 2000 feet — all within 5 miles. If you do not mind strenuous hiking and climbing over fallen trees, the trail is worthwhile as a day hike to the ridge crest or as a loop with the main Rock Creek Trail.

Off-Trail Routes from Arta Lake Road

Adventurous hikers can find several cross-country scrambling routes from the Arta Lake Road to the Wilderness Boundary on the crest of East Grandaddy Mountain. The drainage is walled by cliffs and good route-finding and a topographic map will be needed.

Rock Creek Trailhead

Destination	Miles One Way	Elevation Gain
Wilderness Boundary	2 1/2	50
Squaw Basin	8	2500
Tworoose Pass	9	2700
West Highline Trail Junction	11	1900
Lightning Lake, Upper Basin	13 1/2	2800
Rocky Sea Pass	13 3/4	3300
East Fork of Bear Pass	15 1/2	3600
East Highline Trail Junction	12 1/2	2900
Dead Horse Pass	13 3/4	3600

USGS Maps: Hayden Peak, Explorer Peak, Tworoose Pass

The Rock Creek Trail fans out into three areas: Grandaddy Basin, Upper Rock Creek, and Squaw Basin. This is a huge drainage and Wilderness visitors enter it from several trailheads. A trail follows the river from the trailhead at the Upper Stillwater Reservoir all the way to the head of Rock Creek.

The Highline Trail crosses this drainage going from Rocky Sea Pass to Dead Horse Pass and offers a shorter access to the upper reaches of the Rock Creek drainage. Squaw Basin sits up on the east side above Rock Creek and can be reached from the Brown Duck Trail by hiking over Tworoose Pass. Rock Creek is not the recommended access to Grandaddy Basin as the Grandview Trailhead starts much higher.

The Rock Creek Trailhead is located at the Upper Stillwater Reservoir. A paved road goes from Mountain Home to the Trailhead. To get there, head north from Duchesne. Continue north to a junction just beyond a hairpin turn where the road crosses a drainage. The road to Mountain Home branches north 15.6 miles from the US 40 turnoff and Highway 87 continues east toward Altamont. Turn west onto a paved road at a junction 18.1 miles from Duchesne. There is a country store on this corner and a sign points to Upper Stillwater Reservoir. The paved road continues another 23.2 miles to the Wilderness trailhead, which is on the west side of the dam. The gravel road to Arta Lake and Hanna heads west from the paved road just before the trailhead. Rock Creek Trailhead is a modern, improved trailhead. It has a trailhead host, parking for about 20 cars, and picnic tables.

Rock Creek, Brown Duck Basin
Lake Fork River

← See Map Page 93

The road between Mountain Home and the trailhead crosses private and Tribal land for the first 15 miles. Beyond the Ashley Forest boundary there are two campgrounds and numerous informal campsites.

Rock Creek Trail (#069)

The trail starts at the northwest end of the parking area and a well-constructed trail goes up the hill and past the west end of the Stillwater dam. The trail has been blasted and carved out of the steep hillside above the reservoir and is not as pleasant and the old trail — now submerged. At the upper end of the reservoir it goes into the trees, enters the Wilderness and continues up the drainage.

The Rock Creek Trail leads up past the West Fork junction at 3 miles, and past Squaw Basin junction 4 miles from the start. Farther along is the Fall Creek junction to Phinney and Ledge Lakes. The Fall Creek Trail leads to the junction with the Highline Trail on the east side of Rock Creek and is the route to Dead Horse Pass. The main trail follows Rock Creek in a northwest direction, crosses the Highline Trail on the west side of the drainage and continues to the upper basin and ends at Helen Lake.

The beginning is a boring trail; you don't even see Rock Creek, but you can hear it down in the gorge below. The trail goes along above the stream, through a tunnel of timber. It is a gradual climb with no passes or high points. You pass through a large area that burned in the mid-1970s and is now regenerating. There are many campsites along the floor of this long canyon that can be used on the first or last night of a backpack. Streams come down occasionally so drinking water is no problem.

At the Highline Trail it starts to open up a little and there are a few meadows where you can start to see the spectacular peaks ahead. But it's worth it—once you get into upper Rock Creek, you are near the timberline in beautiful alpine basin country.

The upper extension of the Rock Creek Trail continues for 4 miles after it crosses the Highline Trail and ends at Helen Lake where it joins the Head of Rock Creek Trail. About 2 miles north of the Highline Trail you will reach a trail junction. Black Lake is 1/2 mile southwest, Ouray Lake is 1/4 mile east, and Jack and Jill Lakes are 1/2 mile east. Continuing north, you'll reach Lightning Lake in 1 1/2 miles. Another 1/2 mile will bring you to the Head of Rock Creek Trail at Helen Lake.

On the main Rock Creek Trail you climb about 2,000 feet in 17 miles; however, the last mile and a half is pretty steep, so the rest of the trail is a relatively slow climb. Horses chop up the trail, but it's not bad hiking. The trails in this area are not nearly as good as those in Grandaddy Basin but all are well-used and passable.

West Fork Trail (or LaMarla Lake Trail) (#073)

It's a gentle climb for 3 miles up Rock Creek to the West Fork junction where a steel bridge gets you across the stream if you wish to go to Grandaddy Basin. Some people go in at Grandaddy and come out at Stillwater. It's possible to make the 18 miles in two days, but it's a better three or four day trip.

Highline Trail - Rocky Sea Pass to Dead Horse Pass

The Highline Trail crosses the upper Rock Creek and can be reached from either the Rock Creek Trail on the west side or from the Fall Creek and Ledge Trails on the east side of the drainage.

The Highline Trail enters the Rock Creek drainage from the west across Rocky Sea Pass at 11,250 feet. The trail descends switchbacks down a steep boulder-covered slope dropping 500 feet in 1/4 mile. At the bottom of the steep section there is a junction with the Head of Rock Creek Trail, a spectacular loop to the north around the upper basins that rejoins the Highline Trail. Continue on the Highline Trail through the lake and meadow area below the pass and drop down into heavy timber for about 3/4 mile, then descend to the junction with the main Rock Creek Trail at the river.

The Highline Trail going east between the main Rock Creek Trail and Ledge Lake is a well-worn trail going through open country around patches of timber. Continuing east on the Highline Trail, about 2 miles beyond the Rock Creek Trail you reach an important trail junction. The right fork (north) is the other end of the Head of Rock Creek Trail.

Ledge Lake, near the trail junction, has abundant campsites at the lake and in the meadow to the east. Fall Lake is a small lake (1 acre) located west of Ledge Lake below the Highline Trail. This lake is due south of a prominent ridge. It also has good camping.

Going north from Ledge Lake on the Highline Trail, it's a gradual climb until you get directly east of Continent Lake, about 1 3/4 miles from Ledge.

From directly east of Continent Lake the trail switches almost straight up the talus slope. The pass is on the backbone of the Uinta Mountains. From the top at 11,600 feet, the trail switches down the other side to Dead Horse Lake. The section of the trail down from the pass is extremely steep and hazardous, especially for horses. Riders are advised to get off and lead their horses.

This is the only section of the Highline Trail on the north of the Uintas divide. At Dead Horse Lake it joins the West Fork of Blacks Fork Trail, swings across to the northeast, and climbs to Red Knob Pass at 12,000 feet where it crosses back into the Lake Fork drainage on the south side.

Continent Lake Cross-Country

There is no trail leading into Continent Lake. It is at the southern base of the climb to Dead Horse Pass, enclosed in a cirque where the mountain bends south. Just head off to the west about 1/2 mile across open country to the lake. It is good fishing, but campsites are open and exposed to storms.

Squaw Basin Area

Squaw Basin Trail to Cleveland Pass (#063)

Squaw Basin is good if you want a shorter trip than going all the way up Rock Creek. The area has many lakes and is not as heavily used as Grandaddy Basin. From a camp in Squaw Basin you can make a day hike to timberline at Cleveland Pass.

At the Squaw Creek junction there is a bridge across the stream. From here to Squaw Basin is 6 miles up steep switchbacks and through a burnt area for a couple of miles. Squaw Basin is fairly open, with meadows and timber running together. You will pass through Big Meadows, a very large meadow with a stream meandering through the eastern part. There is an excellent spring right alongside the trail at Big Meadow. The spring is very small, about a foot across, with clear cold water coming out. A trail junction here gives you the choice of going southeast to Tworoose Pass, or north around the Squaw Basin Loop.

Squaw Basin Loop (#063, #066, #121)

About 1/2 mile north of Big Meadows is another junction. Straight ahead leads to upper Rock Creek on the Ledge Trail. To the right is a loop that goes around Squaw Basin and back to the Ledge Trail. From the loop you can continue east to Cleveland Pass and Ottoson Basin or go southeast across Tworoose Pass.

Cleveland Pass is reached by going east from the Squaw Basin loop trail just before Squaw Lake. The trail follows Squaw Basin Creek and along the base of Brown Duck Mountain. It's not difficult to reach the pass but it is a steady climb, going up 1000 feet in 3 miles. The pass is in open country above timberline at 11,200 feet. At Cleveland Lake, just short of the pass, the East Basin Trail coming from Lake Fork joins from the southeast. Beyond Cleveland Pass is Ottoson Basin in the Lake Fork drainage.

Squaw Lake is reached on the loop trail after climbing up about 700 feet for 2 1/2 miles. It is a shallow lake (10 acres) with good camping spots, and contains trout. Shamrock Lake is inside the loop trail and is best reached by cross-country hiking from the west. The best campsites are west of Shamrock in the meadows.

Rock Lakes Spur

Rock Lakes lie in the upper part of Squaw Basin against the base of the mountain. This short trail starts near where the loop rejoins the Ledge Trail about 1 1/2 miles above Big Meadow. Here the Ledge Trail takes off away from the stream and climbs to the west and the Rock Lakes Trail goes north.

It's about a mile up to the first lake, passing a boggy area and occasionally going through heavy timber. Both lakes are fairly small and have good camping in the meadows to the south.

Tworoose Pass Trail (#065)

At the trail junction in Big Meadow, the trail to the east will take you up to Tworoose Pass and out of Squaw Basin. Continuing across Tworoose Pass, the trail will bring you to Kidney Lake, Brown Duck Lake, and on to the Lake Fork Trailhead. A well-marked connecting trail branches north 1 mile from Big Meadow and is an alternative route to Cleveland Pass.

Off-Trail Hiking West of Tworoose Pass

From the north side of Tworoose Pass (before crossing), you can drop back to the west a short distance to Rudolph Lakes which lie along the northern base of the mountain. This is a series of three lakes, upper, middle and lower, the lower being the largest (26 acres). All three have campsites and have been stocked with brook trout.

From Lower Rudolph Lake, you can hike on down the drainage to Mid and farther to Diamond Lake. Mid Lake is quite small (5 acres) and shallow, so fish winter kill. Diamond Lake is larger (13 acres) and deep enough to sustain fish through the winter.

There is no trail to the above lakes; you just follow the drainage from one to the next. For hikers this is no problem. Horses may have problems getting around the fallen trees. Continuing down from Diamond, you end up back at Big Meadow in Squaw Basin.

Horseshoe Lake

Between Diamond Lake and Big Meadow in Squaw Basin, there is a route going 1 mile south to Horseshoe Lake. This small (3 acres) lake gets very little pressure from campers or anglers. It sits right against the base of the mountain and is surrounded by boulders and scattered timber. It has camping places and is stocked with brook trout. It may also be reached by going west a little over 1/2 mile from Diamond Lake.

Ledge Trail (#121)

This trail is reached by starting north around the Squaw Basin loop from Big Meadow and in about 1 1/2 miles taking the left fork. The north end of the Squaw Basin Loop continues to the right from this junction. On the Ledge Trail it is 7 miles to Phinney Lake and 10 to the head of Rock Creek. Turn left on the Ledge Trail and you start a steep climb up to the ridge, about 1/2 mile above. Once on the ridge, your heavy climbing is finished for many miles.

Continuing on the Ledge Trail, it's a gradual climb on only a fair trail. It's marked with tree blazes in the timber and rock cairns in the open areas. The trail follows along the base of a boulder-covered slope. It goes in and out of the timber and has several boggy areas where springs come out from under the boulders. This section is mostly open country; you overlook Rock Creek and can easily see across the valley. You will have no problem following it for the first 3 miles, but the last 1 1/2 miles you'll need to keep a close watch for the trail.

As you get close to Anderson Lake from Ledge Trail, watch carefully for the blazes and cairns. Going up the trail it's easier to stay on it, going down is more difficult. Usually you can see from one marker to the next. If you try to go where you think the trail is, you may get off the trail. Be sure you spot the next marker before proceeding.

Anderson Lake sits near the end of Fall Creek in partly timbered country. It is average sized (6 acres) and is stocked with trout. This lake can be approached from Rock Creek to the south, Moon Lake to the west, and Buck Pasture on West Fork of Blacks Fork from the north.

About 1/4 mile north of Anderson Lake is Phinney Lake, near the junction of the Fall Creek Trail with Ledge Trail. It is about a mile southeast of where the Ledge Trail joins the Highline Trail. Phinney Lake (14 acres) sits at the head of one of the branches of Fall Creek in fairly open country with plenty of good campsites.

Upper Rock Creek
Dave Wallace Photo

Near Phinney Lake the Ledge Trail joins the upper end of the Fall Trail. Ledge Lake lies at the end of Ledge Trail where it joins the Highline Trail. From here it's 20 miles to Mirror Lake, 8 miles over Dead Horse Pass to Buck Pasture in the West Fork of Blacks Fork, and about 13 miles to the Rock Creek Trailhead down Fall Creek. The lake is small (3 acres), sitting against low rock ledges on the north side. It has been stocked with brook trout. There are several good campsites near the lake.

Fall Creek Trail (#171)

This trail leaves the main Rock Creek Trail 8 miles above the trailhead and follows Fall Creek for 4 long miles to Phinney Lake where it joins the Ledge Trail. It's a steep, steady climb, gaining 1,400 feet in elevation. The trail passes the waterfalls that give the trail its name and climbs through an area of spectacular rock formations eroded from soft shale.

Upper Rock Creek Area

Most hikers enter upper Rock Creek by crossing Rocky Sea Pass rather than coming up Rock Creek. The trail from Mirror Lake is shorter and the route from Grandview is more scenic. However you get there, once you're near the top the scenery is so fantastic that you forget the weight of the pack on your back.

Snow at Rocky Sea and Dead Horse passes makes foot travel difficult earlier than mid-July. Contact a ranger regarding snow conditions before planning an early season trip.

Head of Rock Creek Trail (#122)

The west end of this trail begins near the base of Rocky Sea Pass and, staying high, follows around the edge of upper Rock Creek basin. It is one of the most scenic trails in the entire Wilderness. It traverses the bowl at timberline, giving views of the entire Rock Creek drainage below and the crest of the Uinta Mountains above. Using the Head of Rock Creek Trail combined with the Highline Trail you can do a number of great day-hike loops from a base camp. Since the Highline is described west to east, the Head of Rock Creek is described in the opposite direction.

The Head of Rock Creek Trail is in poor condition. But it is marked with rock cairns and blazes and the country is open enough so you can usually spot the next cairn off in the distance if you should wander off the trail. This trail is not dangerous, but some care should be exercised as you pass near the cliffs and ledges. Off-trail hiking may get you hung up on a ledge.

The east end of the Head of Rock Creek Trail joins the Highline Trail about 1 1/2 miles west of Ledge Lake in fairly level open country.

About a mile or so from the Highline Trail on the Head of Rock Creek Trail you can head north for Jodie, Doug, Boot, and Reconnaissance Lakes. There are no trails leading to them. You will have no trouble finding them if you just take off cross-country, following up the streams. They are all in open country in the cirque at the base of the Uinta crest. They range in size from 2 acres to 11 at about 11,500 feet elevation. Most of them contain trout and have exposed camping for backpackers. The area is somewhat boggy in places due to the many springs and streams.

Jack and Jill Lakes are just below the side trail that runs parallel to the Head of Rock Creek Trail. Both lakes are surrounded by timber and have campsites and fishing.

Lightning Lake area from ridge between Rock Creek and Amethyst Lake
Dave Wallace Photo

Helen Lake sits right against the base of the Uinta crest in a rocky meadow, with a few trees and low brush opposite the cliffs. You will find some sheltered campsites here. A small ridge separates Lightning Lake from Helen Lake. Both are very scenic glacial lakes with spectacular cliffs and ridges above them. The north extension of the main Rock Creek Trail joins the Head of Rock Creek Trail between Helen and Lightning Lakes.

Going west on the Head of Rock Creek Trail beyond the end of the main Rock Creek Trail near Lightning Lake you immediately begin a steep climb back onto the upper bench. (Watch carefully for the rock cairns.) You stay on this bench for about a mile.

From here you get the most complete view of the mountains around you and the entire Rock Creek drainage below. To the east you can see Explorer Peak, Squaw Peak, and Cleveland Peak, and the long ridge that defines the northwest edge of Squaw Basin. Behind you to the northwest is Ostler Peak at 12,672 feet. To the south from Spread Eagle Peak is the jagged ridge line containing Rocky Sea Pass, about 4 miles away. You can see Gladys Lake below you to the right and soon you climb down off the upper bench to pass above this lake. Here you are right at timberline and pass through patches of brush and stunted trees.

The Head of Rock Creek Trail passes just below Rosalie Lake, which sits against the base of the mountain with Margie Lake just to the southwest of it. These lakes sit in open glacial cirques in beautiful alpine surroundings. The area contains many small streams and springs but there are high spots where you can camp.

An unmaintained trail from Margie goes south past Uintah Lake and around the point of the mountain and is an alternative route to the base of Rocky Sea Pass. Uintah Lake lies about 1/2 mile south of Margie and has a few campsites.

At Rosalie Lake, the Head of Rock Creek Trail turns east and starts down. It descends steeply to Black Lake, hidden in the timber. From here the trail is fairly level through timber with occasional openings. Brinkley Lake is just before the Highline Trail junction.

East Fork of Bear River from Helen Lake

Following the Head of Rock Creek Trail east from Helen Lake for about 1/2 mile brings you to where a cross-country route takes off east then north to a pass. There was once a trail but it is very little used, so it may be difficult to follow. You cross a wide basin along the main Uintas divide and then climb about 800 feet in about a mile to the pass at 11,600 feet. The abandoned trail crosses over and drops down to Priord Lake at the end of the East Fork of Bear River Trail.

Amethyst Lake Overlook from Helen Lake

You can hike northwest from Helen Lake to reach a low point on the ridge just west of Ostler Peak and overlooking Amethyst Lake in the Stillwater drainage. There seems to be some inconsistency regarding which point on the ridge is named "Ostler Pass" but both this overlook and the route from Helen Lake to the East Fork of the Bear are worthwhile hikes up to the ridge.

I went to the woods because I wished to live deliberately, to front only the essential facts of life, and see if I could not learn what it had to teach, and not, when I came to die, discover that I had not lived.

— Henry David Thoreau

Lake Fork Trailhead (Moon Lake)

Two major trails start here. The most heavily used is the route to the numerous lakes in Brown Duck Basin and branching west to Tworoose Pass and Squaw Basin, and north to East Basin and Ottoson Basin. The other main trail goes directly up along the river for many miles before joining the Highline Trail at the base of Mount Lovenia. The Highline Trail runs across the head of Lake Fork from Red Knob Pass to Porcupine Pass.

There are two loop trails that are popular four-day backpacking trips. The first goes up Brown Duck Trail, over Tworoose Pass, to Squaw Basin, on to Cleveland Pass, returning through East Basin to Brown Duck Basin and back to Moon Lake. The second goes up the Brown Duck Trail to East Basin, to Cleveland Pass, into Ottoson Basin, down Ottoson Creek to the Lake Fork Trail, then down it to Moon Lake. They are pretty much the same distance, about 32 miles. Taking the Squaw Basin route, you are in high country, most of the time right near timberline. The Ottoson Basin route is in the high country half the time but coming down Lake Fork for the last 10 miles is like being in a tunnel of tall timber.

Moon Lake, nearly 800 acres, is the largest lake in the Uinta Mountains. It is an active reservoir so the shoreline fluctuates. It is a beautiful lake surrounded by timber on three sides, with a sandy beach near the public camping area.

To get to the Lake Fork Trailhead, head north from US 40 in Duchesne on Utah 87 following signs toward Mountain Home. Continue north to a junction just beyond a hairpin turn where the road crosses a drainage. The road to Mountain Home branches north 15.6 miles from the US 40 turnoff and Highway 87 continues east toward Altamont. Continue north on the paved road through Mountain Home. North of Mountain Home, 18.9 miles north of Duchesne, the road jogs right for 0.1 mile then turns left and continues north. Just beyond the jog the pavement ends and a gravel road continues north across Tribal land (no hiking or camping). There is a major junction 3.7 miles beyond the end of the pavement. Here the road to Yellowstone turns right and crosses a bridge and the road to Moon Lake goes straight. The Moon Lake road is wide and well maintained. All turnoffs are clearly secondary roads. The road crosses the National Forest boundary and the pavement starts again 4.8 miles beyond the turnoff to Yellowstone. The Lake Fork Trailhead parking area is on the left 4.7 miles beyond the Ashley Forest boundary and 32.8 miles from Duchesne.

The trailhead parking is about 1/2 mile south of the actual end of the road at the Moon Lake Campground. The start is a bit confusing since there are a lot of roads and informal trails in the area. A path leads north from the trailhead following a power line. One start for the Brown Duck Basin Trail is found about 100 yards down the power line from the trailhead. The path continues along the power line right of way for about 10 minutes, loops behind the campground, crosses the road leading to the guard station right at the edge of the campground, and continues a short way to the lake shore. Here the Lake Fork Trail goes north along the lake shore. The other start of the Brown Duck hiking trail immediately branches left and heads up hill.

Brown Duck Trail (#062)

Destination	Miles One Way	Elevation Gain
Wilderness Boundary	3	1200
Brown Duck Lake	6 1/2	2100
Tworoose Pass	10	2600
East Basin Pass	10 1/2	2600
East Basin	13 1/2	-400 from pass
Cleveland Pass	15	3500
Ottoson Basin	16 1/2	-600 from pass

USGS Maps: Kidney Lake, Tworoose Pass, Oweep Creek

There are two starts for the Brown Duck Trail: the mine road route and the hiking route. The hiking trail branches from the Lake Fork Trail on the lake shore just north of the campground and climbs steeply through timber above the stream for about a mile to where it joins the old mine road.

The mine road starts 100 yards north of the parking area, climbs directly up the hill and then levels off and continues north. Following the mine road for 1 1/2 miles brings you to a junction with the Brown Duck hiking trail where there is a registration box. The combined trail going west is an old road, used to build and repair the (now breached) dam at Brown Duck Lake.

The trail leaves Slate Creek (which it has been following) and crosses the tip of a ridge, with a good view of Moon Lake below. After another 1/2 mile, you reach the Wilderness boundary sign. You descend to Brown Duck Creek and follow it up to the lake.

Brown Duck Lake is surrounded by timber and small meadows, as are all the lakes in the basin. The old dam has been breached and the lake is no longer used to store water. The shoreline is not very attractive in its present drawn-down condition, leaving a wide bare ring covered with old logs and stumps all around the lake.

Just before reaching Brown Duck Lake, you come to a major trail junction. The Tworoose Pass Trail begins here and goes northwest past several lakes then across Tworoose Pass into Squaw Basin. The main trail continues north to Clements Lake, crosses East Basin and continues to Cleveland Pass where you can either go down to Squaw Basin in the Rock Creek drainage or go down to Ottoson Basin in the Lake Fork drainage.

Going north from Brown Duck Lake, Atwine Lake is 2 miles away over gently rolling terrain. Atwine is a beautiful natural lake, surrounded by dense forest. It is 32 acres in size, with camping available all around it.

Clements Lake is about 1 1/2 miles from Atwine, along a gently climbing trail. This is a reservoir, about twice as big as Atwine, with a broken earth dam at one end where the trail crosses. There are some excellent campsites on the north side among the trees.

Leaving Clements Lake, the trail continues northwest through timber, passes beautiful open meadows, and crosses a rocky slope to approach East Basin Pass. This is hardly a pass in the usual sense because it is so easy to cross, coming from the south. As you approach the pass through the timber, you suddenly break out into the open and have an outstanding view of the entire upper Lake Fork Basin, clear up to the crest of the Uinta Mountains. This is a good place to stop a moment and, with map and compass, try to identify the different peaks in view. The Lake Fork Trail is below you to the east, but there is no way to get down to it from here.

Dropping from the pass, you quickly lose about 300 feet of elevation, then continue in a northwesterly direction, first along the base of the huge boulder slopes on your left, then out into the beautiful meadow and lake country of East Basin.

East Basin to Cleveland Pass

About 3 miles from East Basin Pass over rolling country, you will reach a group of small lakes. Picture Lake sits off the trail about 1/2 mile to the west. The best way to find it is to follow the stream up to the lake. It is a natural lake, surrounded by timber on three sides, in a scenic setting against the base of the cliffs, where snow usually remains in the shadows through the summer.

Continuing on through East Basin, at the far side you start climbing and continue steadily for about a mile, leaving the timber and getting out in the open near Cleveland Pass. You gain 600 feet in elevation to reach the 11,200 foot pass. This is a fairly steep climb as you approach the top, then it levels off as you cross the open, rounded pass. Here, high on the ridge, you join the trail coming from Squaw Basin to the west. The trail continues north from the pass into Ottoson Basin and down to the Lake Fork Trail.

Branch Trails from the Cleveland Pass Trail

Brown Duck to Tworoose Pass Trail (#065)

The Trail going west begins at Brown Duck Lake and goes past Island, Kidney, and Tworoose Lakes, then across Tworoose Pass and into Squaw Basin in the Rock Creek drainage. Continuing past Brown Duck Lake you will reach Island Lake in about 1/4 mile. This is a reservoir, so it fluctuates through the summer. It is a popular camping and fishing lake.

About 1/4 mile past Island Lake you will reach Kidney Lake. This large lake is also a reservoir, and the water level drops through the summer. It has a sandy beach and lots of room for camping.

Tworoose Lake is a medium-sized (21 acres) natural lake that sits below Tworoose Pass overlooking Brown Duck Basin. It is stocked with cutthroat trout and has good campsites. The lake sits below the trail about a mile west of Kidney Lake and about 1/2 mile below Tworoose Pass.

Tworoose Pass

The climb from Brown Duck Basin to the pass at just over 10,600 feet elevation is only 300 feet stretched over about 1/2 mile. See the Rock Creek section for the continuation into Squaw Basin. Another trail goes south from Tworoose Pass and ascends to the crest of the ridge where it leaves the Wilderness. This is the Dry Ridge Trail that continues for about 14 miles to the Bear Wallow road.

Cleveland Peak and Squaw Peak

Both summits can be reached by off-trail hiking and boulder-hopping from the trail to Cleveland Pass. This is open country and you can use distant views to plan your route.

These beautiful days must enrich all my life.They do not exist as mere pictures...but they saturate themselves into every part of the body and live always.

— John Muir

Lake Fork Trail (#061)

Destination	Miles One Way	Elevation Gain
Wilderness Boundary	3	0
Ottoson Basin	11 1/2	2500
Highline Tail Junction	13 1/2	2300
Red Knob Pass	17	3900
Squaw Pass	20 1/2	3700
Porcupine Pass	22	4200

USGS Maps: Kidney Lake, Oweep Creek, Mount Lovenia, Mount Powell.

This trail runs from the Moon Lake campground up the Lake Fork River for 20 miles to the Highline Trail, just south of Mount Lovenia. From the campground, this trail follows the lake shore a way, crosses a side stream on a good bridge and then heads north past the Wilderness boundary at the far end of Moon Lake. The Lake Fork River flows in a walled gorge most of the way, so the trail stays above the river until just past the junction with Ottoson Trail (13 miles up), then crosses to the east side where it stays to the end. It's a gradual climb all the way on a good trail, but with little chance to see out of the timber. There are new foot bridges where the trail crosses Ottoson Creek and the Lake Fork River.

The upper Lake Fork basin gets most of its use from hikers coming in on the Highline Trail, and hikers coming across the crest from the East Fork or West Fork of Blacks Fork. This is because of the distance involved in coming up the Lake Fork River.

Branch Trails from the Lake Fork Trail

Ottoson Basin Trail (#063)

The trail up Ottoson Creek to about a mile beyond Cleveland Pass is relatively new trail and in good condition. It is 13 miles up to the Ottoson Junction from the Lake Fork Trailhead, then 3 miles into the basin, and another mile to Cleveland Pass. Ottoson Basin consists of mostly open, rocky country with scattered patches of brush and timber. There are several lakes and small streams here. Upper and Lower Ottoson Lakes are in the upper end of the basin.

There are no maintained trails inside Ottoson Basin, but it is surrounded on three sides by mountains and has the Ottoson Trail crossing the fourth side, so one would have difficulty getting lost. Overlooking the basin are three large peaks, Explorer, Squaw, and Cleveland, making the basin a very scenic area to visit. The entire basin is rocky, so only primitive campsites are available. There is sheep grazing here in early summer.

Highline Trail - Red Knob to Porcupine Pass (#025)

Magnificent Mount Lovenia towers above the junction of the Lake Fork and Highline Trails. From here it is 12 miles east to Porcupine Pass leading to the Yellowstone drainage and 4 miles northwest to Red Knob Pass into the Blacks Fork Drainage. Some sections of trail above timberline do not have a distinct tread on the ground. Watch for rock cairns and keep track of landmarks.

On the east side of 12,000 foot Red Knob Pass, there is a trail junction high on the ridge. Going west is the trail down to Dead Horse Lake in the West Fork of Blacks Fork. The north branch traverses below Red Knob and drops steeply down the North Slope into the East Fork of Blacks Fork below Mount Lovenia. The Highline Trail drops south and descends steeply for a mile into the Lake Fork drainage. It then continues along the Lake Fork River through open meadows above timberline for 2 more miles to the next trail junction.

Continuing east on the Highline Trail from the Lake Fork-Highline Trail junction you will climb for 1/2 mile to Lambert Meadow, then you will be above timberline for several miles. Lambert Lake sits below the Highline Trail about a mile east of Lambert Meadow. Cliffs border one side of this 7 acre lake that is right at timberline at 11,000 feet elevation. There are good campsites here.

Past Lambert Lake, you will go around the tip of the ridge and enter Oweep Basin, which contains the headwaters of Oweep Creek. This part of the trail is right at timberline and traverses across the upper part of the basin for about 3 miles to the trail junction with the route to the North Slope across Squaw Pass.

The Highline Trail continues east across Oweep Basin and climbs gradually to the head of the basin, then begins the steep climb to Porcupine Pass. It's about a 600 foot climb in about 1/2 mile to the pass at 12,236 feet. From here you cross over into Garfield Basin in the upper Yellowstone Drainage, and it's 3 miles to Tungsten Lake and Tungsten Pass above it.

Squaw Pass

Just a mile west of Porcupine Pass on the Highline Trail, a trail takes off to the north and climbs to Squaw Pass. It is a little over a mile, past a small lake, and up 600 feet to reach the pass at 11,800 feet. Continuing through the pass, the trail goes down into the Little East Fork of Blacks Fork.

A popular loop is to start at the East Fork of Blacks Fork trailhead, go up the drainage and cross at Red Knob Pass, then take the Highline Trail to Squaw Pass, cross back north into the Little East Fork and return to the trailhead.

Crater Lake Cross-Country Route

Crater Lake, sitting at the base of Explorer Peak, is an interesting side trip for hikers in the upper Lake Fork drainage. There is an informal trail starting about a mile west of the Lake Fork - Highline Trail junction on the Highline Trail. The trail is not maintained and is used mostly by anglers and sheepherders. The lake is a beautiful glacial lake, about 28 acres in size, and is 147 feet deep, the deepest lake in the Uintas. The best camping is about a mile below the lake.

Wilderness Grazing

One of the compromises made to get the original 1964 Wilderness Act passed was to include the dreadful words "the grazing of livestock, where established prior to the effective date of this Act, shall be permitted to continue subject to such reasonable regulations as are deemed necessary by the Secretary of Agriculture." Section 4(d)(4). The Utah Wilderness Act of 1984 contained even stronger wording regarding continuation of prior grazing in Wilderness (Section 301). Grazing is more protected within a Wilderness than it is elsewhere on public land.

These were political compromises. For nearly 30 years environmentalists have had to live with this compromise while listening to ranchers endlessly argue against more Wilderness because it would hurt their operations. Recently I heard a long-time and respected wilderness advocate tell a newly-elected member of Congress "We are getting tired of this and maybe it is time to demand a change."

OWEEP BASIN

Center Park Trailhead

Destination	Miles One Way	Elevation Gain
Wilderness Boundary	2	600
Swasey Lake	5	600
Garfield Basin	9	800
Tungsten Pass & Highline Trail	12 1/2	1200

USGS Maps: Lake Fork Mountain, Garfield Basin

This trail starts at a high elevation and stays high as it crosses the basins and minor ridges along the west edge of the Yellowstone drainage. It is the direct access to the Swasey Lakes area. These lakes sit in very scenic timber country with mountains close above. They have good fishing and campsites and are quite heavily used. Beyond Swasey Lakes the trail goes to Garfield Basin where a connecting trail drops east back to the Yellowstone Trail. The northbound trail continues from Garfield Basin to Tungsten Pass high in the Yellowstone drainage where it joins the Highline Trail.

The trailhead is located near the upper end of Hells Canyon. To reach this canyon from US 40 in Duchesne follow the directions listed below for the Swift Creek Trailhead as far as the Ashley National Forest Boundary. The Hells Canyon Road is on the left 0.2 mile north of the boundary sign and 28.2 miles from the start in Duchesne. Go northwest up Hells Canyon 7.6 miles to where the Mill Park and Center Park roads come together and take the right-hand road. In another 0.2 mile the road forks again and you go left to the trailhead. The trailhead consists of a parking area and signboard. Three trails and a logging road leave from here.

Hells Canyon Road is a gravel road and quite rocky, but passenger cars can make it; just don't drive too fast. The lower part of Hells Canyon is steep and narrow but higher up there are plenty of sites for car camping.

This area is in a state of flux with logging operations going on, so it gets confusing. Currently the Swasey Hole Trail starts as a primitive road at the left side of the signboard. The road to the right of the signboard leads through some timber sale areas and ends near the Wilderness boundary. The Toquer Lake Trail and the Fish Creek Trail start from the middle of the parking area and head slightly downhill to the meadow visible ahead where they separate.

Swasey Hole Trail (#059)

From the trailhead at 10,000 feet you have a very gradual hike through timber and long open meadows to the Wilderness boundary in about 2 miles. When you reach the boundary, you begin to drop slightly. You then cross a big mountain of boulders, climbing again to 11,000 feet.The trail is very scenic along here as it overlooks Yellowstone Creek, far below. As you get around it, you are above Swasey Hole, and descend rapidly to it. This section is hard for horses.

Swasey Hole has many small lakes and one fairly large one, Swasey Lake (36 acres), which is about a mile off the trail following the stream. This area is heavily timbered, with numerous camping places among the lakes, meadows and occasional bogs.

From Swasey Hole the trail stays fairly level all the way to Five Point Lake. Continuing from Swasey Hole, you pass around the end of a long finger of mountain and approach Garfield Basin. This basin is a wide, long bench area covered with lakes and streams.

Spider Lake sits along the trail surrounded by meadows. It is so named because of its many long narrow arms which extend out through the timber. Bluebell Lake sits slightly above Spider Lake and can be reached by going up the drainage behind Spider. Both these lakes are medium size and sit in very scenic surroundings.

Drift Lake may be reached by going north on the trail from Spider Lake about 1/4 mile, then going cross country. Follow the stream going west towards the mounatain about 1/2 mile. Drift Lake has poor campsites and is a reservoir so it may fluctuate through the summer.

About a mile north of Spider Lake, the Swasey Hole Trail reaches Five Point Lake. This is a large reservoir subject to a 10 foot fluctuation. It is heavily used by hikers and horses as the main camping place in the Garfield Basin. Timber surrounds the lake on three sides, giving good shelter to campers.

There is a trail junction just below the Five Point Lake dam, 15 miles from the Hells Canyon road. The Five Point Lake Trail going down Garfield Creek to Yellowstone Creek (5 miles) heads east from here. On this trail, it is 15 miles back to the Yellowstone Road. Going north from Five Point Lake, it is 3 miles to Tungsten Lake and 10 miles to Anderson Pass.

There are scattered patches of timber, giving way to completely open terrain as you hike north from Five Point Lake. You begin to see the typically subalpine "Krummholz." These are stunted pine or spruce trees, disfigured by strong winds blowing continually from one direction. Another interesting feature of these trees is the thick skirt which grows around their base. This is often hollow inside, providing a sheltered spot for one or two campers. The high open country area overlooks the Yellowstone drainage and has magnificent views of the surrounding peaks.

Superior Lake lies along the trail about 1/2 mile north of Five Point Lake. Little Superior Lake is a short distance above it, up the drainage. Both lakes are above timberline in open, rocky terrain. They contain cutthroat and brook trout but have little attraction as campsites due to the lack of cover.

Doll Lake lies off the trail about a mile northwest of Five Point Lake. It is a glacial lake, sitting in open, rocky country against the mountain. It's a scenic lake, but not desirable for camping or fishing.

About 1/4 mile past Superior Lake, sitting off the trail to the south, is an historic site. A rock building called the Salt House, built before Wilderness designation, was used by sheepherders to store salt for their sheep.

Proceeding north on the Swasey Hole Trail, in about 2 miles you reach Tungsten Lake. This lake sits in the open in very rough rocky country just below Tungsten Pass. Here the Swasey Hole Trail ends as it joins the Highline Trail. North Star Lake lies about 1/2 mile northwest of Tungsten Lake on the Highline Trail. It is about 14 acres in size, sitting in open rocky tundra with poor camping.

Highline Trail - From Tungsten Pass

West to Porcupine Pass

Going west on the Highline Trail it is 4 miles to Porcupine Pass. You climb gradually across the upper end of Garfield Basin to the base of the pass. Here you begin a steep climb, switching upward to the top at 12,236 feet. Continuing to the west, you drop down into Oweep Basin in the Upper Lake Fork drainage.

East to Yellowstone Trail

Going east from Tungsten Lake toward Tungsten Pass on the Highline Trail, the climb is fairly steep, but nothing like the other major passes. It is only 1/4 mile up from the lake, rising less than 200 feet to the 11,400 foot pass. From here you drop slightly, swinging around a point of the mountain into the upper Yellowstone Drainage. In about 1 1/2 miles from Tungsten Pass, you will reach the junction with the Yellowstone Trail.

Toquer Lake Trail

This less-used trail also starts from the Center Park Trailhead. It is unmaintained and may be hard to follow. It heads northwest and drops down to cross Fish Creek, then climbs along the stream to Toquer Lake inside the Wilderness, 3 miles from the trailhead. This lake is the headwater of Fish Creek and drains to Moon Lake. There is good camping near the lake.

Fish Creek Trail

The Fish Creek Trail is a non-Wilderness trail also starting from Center Park. It goes down along the creek for about 6 miles to Moon Lake. The trail is shown on the Forest Service High Uintas Wilderness Map but not on the USGS topographic map. It is a maintained and marked trail.

Head southwest from the trailhead into the meadow and then go along the edge of the trees. Continue south for about 1/4 mile until you come to an opening where the trees are blazed; turn west here and go downhill. The trail passes through a timber sale area. From Cow Park follow the trail 1/2 mile south across a meadow then watch for a sign that may be hard to find in the trees. The trail goes west through the trees and starts dropping faster as it follows the creek. It ends near the Moon Lake dam.

TUNGSTEN LAKE

Swift Creek Trailhead
(Yellowstone River)

Access to the Wilderness Area up either Yellowstone Creek or Swift Creek starts at the Swift Creek Trailhead at the end of the Yellowstone River road. Here Swift Creek flows into the Yellowstone River. These drainages give access to the highest part of the Uinta Range at Kings Peak.

The Swift Creek Trail is quite heavily used by local people going into Farmers and Timothy Lakes, both popular fishing areas. It is also a drier, more scenic route into the upper Yellowstone basin. It stays higher, sometimes along the ridge where you can see the surrounding mountains. You climb fairly fast and even though you are in the timber, you can see the peaks around you. Some sections, especially the climb to Bluebell Pass, are rocky and may be difficult for horses.

The Yellowstone Trail follows the creek all the way and is a rather wet trail with several stream crossings and boggy areas. Between the Yellowstone Trail and the Swift Creek Trail you have a choice of being in the mud or being on the rocks on your way to the upper Yellowstone basin.

To get to Swift Creek, head north from US 40 in Duchesne on Utah 87 following signs toward Mountain Home. Continue north to a junction just beyond a hairpin turn where the road crosses a drainage. The road to Mountain Home branches north 15.6 miles from the US 40 turnoff and Highway 87 continues east toward Altamont. Continue straight north on the paved road through Mountain Home. North of Mountain Home, 18.9 miles from Duchesne, the road jogs right for 0.1 mile then turns left and continues north. Just beyond the jog the pavement ends and a gravel road continues north across Tribal land.

There is a major junction 3.7 miles beyond the end of the pavement and 23.6 miles from US 40. Here the road to Yellowstone turns right and crosses a bridge and the road to Moon Lake goes straight. Cross the bridge, and in 0.2 mile there is another junction. The road left is the route north to Yellowstone and the road to the right is an alternative route back to the Altamont and Roosevelt area. Turn left and continue another 3.9 miles across Tribal land to the National Forest boundary. The Hells Canyon road to the Center Park Trailhead branches left 0.2 mile beyond the Forest Service boundary and the road to Yellowstone continues straight. Continue past the Yellowstone Campground and cross another bridge. Just beyond the bridge the Yellowstone road turns left and

Swift Creek is the higher, dryer, and more scenic route to upper Yellowstone.
John Veranth Photo

the road to a hydro power plant turns right. The forest road that goes east to the Dry Gulch access and on to Uinta Canyon branches right 1 mile beyond the bridge. Continue straight past the Yellowstone Ranch (private) and past the Reservoir Campground to the trailhead a total of 35.3 miles from US 40. It is a wide, well-maintained gravel road from Mountain Home to the trailhead.

The trailhead has a large parking area with facilities for unloading horses and a Forest Service campground. The Wilderness boundary is just beyond the parking area. The trail starts at the signboard and the Swift Creek and Yellowstone Trails separate after about 100 yards. The Swift Creek Trail heads right and begins a series of switchbacks up the ridge separating the two creeks while the Yellowstone Trail stays low.

Yellowstone Creek Trail (#057)

Destination	Miles One Way	Elevation Gain
Garfield Basin	12	2700
Highline Trail	14 1/2	2800
Anderson Pass	17 1/2	4400

USGS Maps: Burnt Mill Spring, Lake Fork Mountain, Garfield Basin, Mount Powell

The Yellowstone Trail follows the main drainage to join the Highline Trail in the upper basin. It crosses the creek four times with only one bridge. Because of the width of the stream, people have to wade across. This has always been a wet trail but after the wet season in 1986 there was a mud slide that caused the stream to move out into a meadow, flooding part of the former trail. Several beaver dams also are problems, as they cause wet, boggy areas along the trail. The route is flagged through the wet area but in the spring it can be very difficult for hikers and impossible for horses.

Hikers will find the Center Park Trailhead offers a higher, dryer, and shorter route to Five Point Lake. The Swift Creek Trail to Bluebell Pass is a better hiking route to the Anderson Pass area.

The Yellowstone Trail has no steep sections until you reach the junction with the Five Point Lake Trail going up Garfield Creek, 10 miles from the trailhead. The Yellowstone Trail continues north for about 3 miles to a junction with the trail coming across Bluebell Pass from Swift Creek to the east.

You begin climbing along Yellowstone Creek as you approach the upper basin. Near the end the trail climbs more steeply to join the Highline Trail. Here, you're above timberline with an unexcelled view in all directions. Kings Peak and South Kings Peak are in plain view to the east, just south of Anderson Pass.

There is a four-way junction at the Highline Trail. Continuing north is the trail to Smiths Fork Pass. Turn right on the Highline Trail and you will reach Anderson Pass in about 3 miles. West on the Highline Trail leads to Tungsten Pass on an intermediate ridge within the Yellowstone drainage then on to Porcupine Pass where the Highline Trail crosses into the Lake Fork drainage.

Highline Trail - Porcupine Pass to Anderson Pass

Highline Trail East to Anderson Pass

Turning northeast on the Highline Trail from the Yellowstone Trail you will cross the headwaters of Yellowstone Creek and climb to Anderson Pass, at 12,600 feet, in about 3 1/2 miles. There are numerous places to camp along the streams in this area, some in the open, many in the timber. Many hikers use this area as a base camp for climbing Kings Peak. The route up Kings Peak is described in the Henrys Fork section since most hikers approach that way.

Highline Trail West to Porcupine Pass

The Highline Trail is fairly obvious across these upper drainages and is marked with large rock cairns. The trail heads southwest for 1 1/2 miles of gentle climbing to Tungsten Pass where the trail up Garfield Basin joins the Highline Trail. From this junction near Tungsten Lake it is 4 more miles to Porcupine Pass. You pass North Star Lake, climbing gradually across the upper end of Garfield Basin, to the base of the pass. Here you begin a steep climb, up switchbacks to the top at 12,236 feet. Continuing to the west, you drop down into Oweep Basin in the Upper Lake Fork drainage.

North to Smiths Fork Pass (#054)

Going north from the four-way junction is a trail that continues for 3 miles to the Smiths Fork Pass. It's a steady but gradual climb to the elevation of the pass and has no really steep climbing at the top. This pass, at 11,700 feet, crosses over into the East Fork of Smiths Fork and joins the trail coming up from Red Castle Lakes.

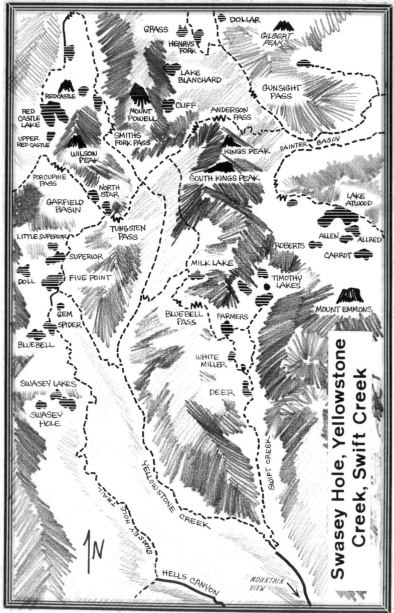

Swasey Hole, Yellowstone
Creek, Swift Creek

Trails Branching from the Yellowstone Trail

Five Point Lake Trail (#058)

This trail starts from the Yellowstone Trail about 10 miles from the trailhead. It is 5 miles long, climbing up Garfield Creek and gaining about 1700 feet to Five Point Lake in Garfield Basin. Although Garfield Basin is part of the Yellowstone drainage it is described from the Center Park Trailhead since that is a shorter and dryer route to the basin.

Farmers Lake Trail (#055)

The Farmers Lake Trail connects the Yellowstone Trail with the Swift Creek area to the east across Bluebell Pass. It branches east about 12 miles from the trailhead, goes northeast to Milk Lake then doubles back to the southwest before finally climbing to Bluebell Pass. Going east from here, it is 2 miles to Milk Lake, 4 miles to Bluebell Pass, and 6 miles to Farmers Lake.

Swift Creek Trail (#056)

Destination	Miles One Way	Elevation Gain
Deer Lake	5	2000
East Timothy Lake	8 1/2	2800
Bluebell Pass	9 1/4	3400
Yellowstone Trail Junction	13	-1600 from pass
Highline Trail via Main Trails	16	4500
Anderson Pass via High Route	16 1/2	5200

USGS Maps: Burnt Mill Spring, Garfield Basin, Mount Emmons

This is a high and dry trail that climbs high on the ridge then drops back to the stream and continues up then branches to Farmers Lake and to Timothy Lake. A connecting route across Bluebell Pass leads to the Yellowstone Trail and a cross-country route leads to the upper basin. This is a shorter and better route for hikers going to upper Yellowstone. The Yellowstone and Swift Creek Trails start at the same point. Just after crossing a bridge the trails separate and the Swift Creek trail heads right.

There are many switchbacks as the trail climbs to the top of the ridge overlooking Yellowstone Creek. Then it becomes less steep as the trail continues above Swift Creek for a way before losing a little elevation to cross the creek. After 5 miles you will reach Deer Lake, a reservoir surrounded by timber with marginal campsites.

Up the trail above Deer Lake 1/2 mile, the trail branches. There are a lot of nice campsites beyond this point. The right branch brings you to Timothy Lakes in 3 miles. The left branch goes to Farmers Lake and continues on to Bluebell Pass and the Yellowstone Trail. The Timothy Lakes branch goes through a couple of meadows then reaches the dam at East Timothy Lake, a large lake right at timberline where Swift Creek has its beginning.

There are many lakes in this basin which may be discovered by following the drainage up from East Timothy. Camping and fishing are good at many of them. Several of the lakes were enlarged by dams constructed before this area was designated as Wilderness. The entire basin is near timberline and offers open meadows with views of boulder-covered ridges above.

Trails Continuing from Upper Swift Creek

Timothy Lakes to Farmers Lake Trail (#055)

A connecting trail between Farmers Lake and Timothy Lakes takes off to the west near the end of the prominent ridge southwest of East Timothy Lake. It is about 1 1/2 mile between the lakes. This trail makes a nice day-hiking loop for backpackers who are camping in the basin. The other end is near the Farmers Lake outlet.

Timothy Lakes to Jackson Park Trail (#055)

A trail starts south from the east end of the Timothy Lake dam and follows the occasional scars of a road cut remaining from the dam construction access. This trail heads south along the east side of the drainage, climbs high onto the south ridge of Mount Emmons, leaves the Wilderness, and ends at Jackson Park. The undeveloped Jackson Park Trailhead can be reached by a primitive road branching from the forest road going between Yellowstone and Uinta Canyon. Access to Jackson Park requires 4WD or at least a high-clearance vehicle.

Mount Emmons Ridge

A long ridge leads south from Kings Peak to Mount Emmons and beyond. From north of East Carroll Lake you can scramble up a long, very steep slope covered with boulders and reach the rounded grass-covered ridge crest overlooking Atwood Basin. Mount Emmons can be reached by hiking south over the intermediate summit. This route to Mount Emmons requires skill in planning your route up through the loose rock and cliffs to the ridge top. The Atwood Basin side is much less steep.

From Swift Creek Trail to Yellowstone (#055)

Two miles from Deer Lake on the left branch trail is White Miller Lake. It is 11 acres in size, and has good camping and fishing. One mile up from White Miller Lake is Farmers Lake, 9 miles from the trailhead. This is the largest (63 acres) of several lakes sitting in a glacial cirque against the base of the peaks. There are a few camping spots around the rocky shore. Bluebell Pass is plainly visible as the low saddle on the ridge west of the lake.

From Farmers Lake, it is a gradual climb up to the base of Bluebell Pass. The final scramble is on steep and rocky switchbacks. This is not recommended for horses but is not a big problem for hikers. At the pass, at 11,600 feet, you have an unobstructed view back down the Swift Creek drainage, and ahead across the upper Yellowstone Creek basin. The trail descends to the meadows, then turns right (north) along the base of the mountain.

About 2 miles from Bluebell Pass going north you reach Milk Lake. This lake lies about 1/8 mile off the trail in a scenic glacial cirque. Its name was derived from its murky appearance. This is caused by glacial dust which was formed when glaciers ground boulders together. It is still seeping out from under the boulders around the lake after all these years. A rock dam still stands across the end of the lake, but it no longer holds back the water. This lake has been stocked with brook trout — it is worth a try. There are some beautiful campsites west and south of the lake.

The trail drops down from below the lake to a large open meadow where you turn left and follow the edge for a way. Here, a cross-country route heads north to the upper basin and the main trail continues southwest and rather steeply down about 2 miles to join the Yellowstone Trail.

Milk Lake to Upper Yellowstone Basin

This is a cross-country route, not a trail. Tread softly as you pass through this pristine area. It starts in the big meadow below Milk Lake and takes you to the Highline Trail in upper Yellowstone Basin. From the lower end of the big meadow, you go north across the stream and then go back east along the other side of the meadow about half way. Then you swing north, where a gradual climb brings you to the timberline. Continue generally northward, with the mountain base on your right until you reach the Highline Trail. You're in open country with little chance of getting lost.

At the Highline Trail, you can go east to Anderson Pass near Kings Peak and cross into Painter Basin. Going west on the Highline Trail takes you to a four-way trail junction with the main Yellowstone Trail and the trail north to Smiths Fork Pass.

East Timothy Lake and upper Swift Creek Basin / John Veranth Photo

Dry Gulch Access

Destination	Miles One Way	Elevation Gain
Wilderness Boundary	5 1/2	2200
Flat Top Mountain	7	3100

USGS Maps: Burnt Mill Spring, Mount Emmons

The undeveloped trailhead at Dry Gulch can be used to reach the Wilderness boundary high on the south slope of Flat Top Mountain. This trailhead also gives access to the Lowline Trail which leads to a large area of primitive backcountry west of the Uinta Canyon drainage and north of the Tribal land.

To get to Dry Gulch follow the directions for Uinta River Trailhead to the road junction at the end of the pavement 18.5 miles north of Roosevelt. Starting here is a rough gravel road going to Dry Gulch and Yellowstone Canyon. To reach the west end of this road follow the directions for Swift Creek to the road junction 3.6 miles north of the National Forest boundary.

From the junction at the end of the pavement in Uinta Canyon, the road to Dry Gulch climbs up to a high plateau and heads west across Ute Tribal lands for 10.1 miles before entering the Ashley National Forest. The road to Dry Gulch turns north immediately west of the forest boundary sign. Go north for 3.0 miles to an opening where you can park on the right. Up to this point the road is rough but suitable for carefully driven passenger cars. The last mile of road to the point marked with the trailhead symbol on the Forest Service Wilderness map requires high-clearance vehicles.

Flat Top Trail

The trail to Flat Top starts by following the road up beyond the parking area to the road closure gate 1 mile ahead. Continue beyond the gate on a primitive road toward Heller Lake and turn northwest where a non-maintained trail leaves the road at a minor drainage about 1 mile beyond the gate. This trail climbs steadily and reaches timberline near the Wilderness boundary. Flat Top Mountain is the southern end of a system of ridges and plateaus extending south from Kings Peak. This trail is not easy to follow but is a fun challenge. Between Flat Top and Mount Emmons are many opportunities for off-trail exploration at elevations over 12,000 feet.

Lowline Trail

The Lowline Trail runs between the Dry Gulch Access and Big Springs in Uinta Canyon. The branch roads from the county road between Uinta Canyon and Dry Gulch are on Tribal land and are closed to the public, so this trail provides backcountry access to a large block of Ashley National Forest land around Jefferson Park.

The start of the Lowline Trail is confusing but after the first meadow it becomes a well-worn horse trail through the trees. From the passenger car parking area walk up the road about 1/4 mile. Watch for an opening in the trees on the right with a meadow visible across the stream. The trail crosses the stream, passes along the northwest side of a corral in the meadow and enters the trees again on the north side of the clearing. Walk through the aspen aiming for the east side of the ridge ahead and you will soon find a distinct trail on the left side of the stream.

The trail is marked with tree blazes and passes through aspens that are beautiful in the fall. The trail follows the stream for a couple of miles then switchbacks east up to Jefferson Park. Almost directly west across Jefferson Park it drops steeply down into Uinta Canyon. This last section is harder to find.

Uinta River Trailhead

Destination	Miles One Way	Elevation Gain
Wilderness Boundary	3	400
Chain Lakes	7	2800
Lake Atwood	12	3600
Highline Trail - Kidney Lakes	11	2600
Fox Lake	13 1/2	3000

USGS Maps: Bollie Lake, Mount Emmons, Kings Peak, Fox Lake

On the Uinta River, you can drive to within 3 miles of the Wilderness boundary. This large drainage includes Krebs Basin, Chain Lakes, Atwood Basin, Painter Basin, Kidney Lakes, and Fox Basin. Because they are close to the trailhead, Krebs Basin, Chain Lakes and Atwood Basin all get heavy usage.

This drainage is so long and so large that the upper basins are easier to reach from other trailheads. Painter Basin on the far northwest side is 17 miles going up Uinta Canyon but 11 miles from Henrys Fork Trailhead. Fox Lake on the northeast side is only 7 miles from the West Fork of Whiterocks Trailhead.

The Uinta River runs in a deep gorge like most of the South Slope rivers. The gorge is 200 to 300 feet deep in some places. It's nearly impossible to get down to the river from the trail to fish, although the trail parallels the river fairly closely all the way.

A suggested loop for about a 70 mile hike: Go to Chain Lakes the first day; camp at Atwood Lake the second; climb Kings Peak and camp in Painter Basin the third day; camp at Kidney Lakes the fourth day; then return down Uinta River in a very long day.

To get to the Uinta River Trailhead from US 40 in Roosevelt, take Utah 121 which starts at the four-way intersection where US 40 makes a right-angle turn. Follow Utah 121 for 10.1 miles to an intersection in Neola where Utah 121 turns right and heads to Vernal and a paved road to Uinta Canyon continues straight. Between Neola and the Forest Service boundary the road crosses Tribal lands. Side roads branching from the county road are marked with "Tribal Permission Required" signs.

There is another major intersection 7 miles north of Neola where the road to Uinta Canyon continues straight and a road to Whiterocks turns right and makes a hairpin turn across the river.

**Chain Lakes, Uinta River,
Whiterocks River**

← See Map Page 129

The pavement ends in another 1.4 miles at a junction. The right branch is the main road to Uinta Canyon and the left branch is the road to the Dry Gulch Trailhead and on to Yellowstone Canyon.

Continue north another 3.9 miles, take the right branch at Big Springs and cross the Uinta River. Just beyond the bridge there is another junction. The road to Uinta Canyon turns left and enters the Ashley National Forest and the Elkhorn Loop road heads right. The Elkhorn Loop road connects with the road to Chepeta Lake. The trailhead parking is on the left 3.5 miles beyond the Ashley Forest boundary and 26 miles from Roosevelt. Beyond the pavement the road is well-maintained gravel all the way.

The trail officially starts at a large trailhead parking area about 1/2 mile south of the road end. Parking at Smoky Springs just outside the U-Bar Ranch is limited to day use only. The Forest Service has built a trail from the backcountry parking area to the end of the road but walking the road is faster. From the Smoky Springs parking area at the end of the road you can pick up the Uinta River Trail by going slightly uphill to the east corner of the fence around the U-Bar Ranch permit area. There is a livestock-control gate (be sure to close it behind you) and beyond here the trail is distinct and well used.

Within a short distance down the road from the trailhead are four campgrounds: Wandin, Uinta Springs, Uinta Park and Uinta Canyon. The U-Bar Dude Ranch at the road end is an outfitter-guide resort with cabins.

Uinta River Trail (#044, #046)

The Uinta River Trail follows the main drainage. After crossing the Shale Creek bridge the trail splits three ways. One branch turns west and joins the Highline Trail in Painter Basin. The middle trail continues north and joins the Highline Trail east of Kidney Lakes. A branch goes northeast to join the Highline Trail near Fox Lake.

It is about 3 miles to the Wilderness boundary at Sheep Bridge. The trail doesn't climb much as it follows the river through scattered lodgepole pine and meadows. It is not a very good trail as it crosses boggy areas around beaver ponds. It is not difficult—just muddy.

Continuing north from Sheep Bridge, the trail stays above the river, climbing gradually. You cross the Rock Canyon Bridge after 3 miles, then cross Bluebell Creek in about 2 more. About 1 1/2 mile past Bluebell Creek, you will climb high above the river as you approach Shale Creek. You travel on a bench with steep rocky country above and the river gorge below. Soon you reach the shale dugway which is a safety hazard to horses because the trail has a tendency to slide into the river gorge. However, this area presents no problem for hikers.

Just about a mile north of the shale dugway, you will reach the major trail junction. The Uinta River Trail goes west to North Fork Park and continues on to reach the Highline Trail in Painter Basin 10 miles away. Farther north, the Shale-Fox Cutoff takes off to the right going 3 miles to Fox Lake. Continuing north about 2 miles on the main trail you reach the Highline Trail east of Kidney Lakes.

The Uinta River Trail is practically level all the way to North Fork Park (3 miles) where Gilbert Creek joins the Uinta River. Just before reaching the park, a very wet trail takes off to the north and connects with the Highline Trail in about 2 miles. You would take this trail if you wished to go up Gilbert Creek.

From North Fork Park continuing west, the Uinta River Trail follows the river and climbs gradually for about 7 miles to Painter Basin.

Painter Basin is a beautiful alpine basin sitting above timberline at the base of Kings Peak. It is laced throughout with small streams and boggy patches. There are numerous very small lakes; the two or three larger ones are about 6 acres. There is very little shelter from the wind but you can find campsites in patches of trees. Near the lower end of the basin, the Uinta River Trail branches. The right (north) fork is a 1/2-mile connecting trail that crosses to the Highline Trail. From there you can continue west to either Anderson Pass or Gunsight Pass. The main trail continues southwest, climbing across open terrain to the base of the mountain, where you climb to Trail Rider Pass, up about 400 feet of switchbacks in 1/2 mile. The trail south of the pass is described as the Chain Lakes - Atwood Trail.

The maps and trails are somewhat confusing in the upper Uinta Basin. None of the maps is entirely correct. There has been some renaming in this area so maps and trail descriptions do not all agree. The trails across the upper basin are now the Uinta River Trail and the Highline Trail and there is no "North Fork." Gilbert Creek is called the "Center Fork" on some maps.

The maintained trails are marked with rock cairns so you should have little trouble reaching your destination. The middle of the drainage is forested but the upper basins are open country. You can go cross-country as a lot of people do. It is easy to see from point to point if you are at all familiar with the country or have a good map and know how to read it. It's difficult to get lost because you can see landmarks in all directions. Because of cross cutting, the trails get a little hazy in heavily used areas such as in Painter Basin.

Branch Trails from the Uinta River Trail

Shale - Fox Cutoff (#045)

If you take the Shale-Fox cutoff, you reach the Highline Trail in 2 miles. At this junction you're 1 mile from Fox Lake, 5 from Cleveland Lake across the pass to the east, and 3 miles from Kidney Lakes to the west.

Cross-Country Route to Craig and Painter Lakes

At North Fork Park, there is a trail going south around the point of the mountain to Craig Lake and on to Painter Lakes (3 miles). It is a cross-country route to or from the Chain Lakes area and is not a maintained Forest Service trail.

Craig Lake sits just at the mouth of Painter Draw. Painter Lakes are eight lakes in a beautiful basin surrounded on three sides by mountains. Sitting at timberline at 11,000 feet, some of the lakes are in open terrain while others have patches of timber around them, making good camping places. The largest lake is about 14 acres.

To go to Roberts Pass from Craig Lake, the trail (such as it is) goes southeast to get around the point of the mountain south of you. Once around this point, you head southwest crossing Atwood Creek to meet the trail at the base of Roberts Pass.

Chain Lakes - Atwood Basin Trail
Sheep Bridge to Trail Rider Pass

This very popular trail goes up Krebs Creek to Chain Lakes, which are in Krebs Basin, continues to Roberts Pass, crosses into Atwood Basin, passes Atwood Lake to Trail Rider Pass, crosses into Painter Basin and connects with the Uinta River Trail just before the junction with the Highline Trail.

This is primarily a fishing and camping area in high basin country with meadows, timber and rocky ridges interspersed. These basins are in the Uinta River drainage but because of the deep river gorge the access is indirect across a series of intermediate ridges.

From the Uinta River Trailhead it is 3 miles to Sheep Bridge where the Chain Lakes to Atwood Lake Trail branches west from the Uinta River Trail, 1/2 mile south of the Wilderness boundary.

This trail is fairly new and in good condition. It's a hard climb from the bridge to Krebs Basin. You gain 3000 feet in 4 miles.

Krebs Basin is about 6 miles from the Uinta River and about 10 miles from the trailhead. It sits at the base of Mount Emmons, which at 13,440 feet towers almost 3000 feet above this area. There are many small streams and lakes in the upper part of the basin, but no maintained trails to them. You just go cross-country. It would be difficult to get lost as there are mountains on three sides and the trail crossing the fourth.

Lower Chain Lake, about 11 miles from the trailhead, is the first large lake (20 to 60 acres) you reach on this trail. Middle Chain Lake (14 acres) is up the trail, right next to Lower Chain Lake. Upper Chain Lake is just past Middle Chain Lake and about a mile on the trail from Lower Chain Lake. These lakes are mostly below timberline at 10,600 feet but are open enough so you are not in timber all the time.

CHAIN LAKES

You climb about 300 feet on the trail in 1/4 mile to reach 4th Chain Lake. It is about 13 acres in size, and has camping places. The Chain Lakes are closed to horse camping to allow vegetation to recover but horses can stay higher in Krebs Basin.

Oke Doke Lake is a popular fishing spot, lying at the head of the basin 1 mile west of the trail to Roberts Pass. It is in an open cirque at the base of Mount Emmons.

From 4th Chain Lake you'll climb another 400 feet to Roberts Pass, where you cross into Atwood Basin and switchback down about 700 feet. At the northern base of the climb to Roberts Pass there is a cross-country route going over to Painter Lakes.

Atwood Basin is another large glacial basin similar to Krebs Basin, sitting at timberline at the base of Mount Emmons. It has several large lakes, with streams, open meadows and boggy areas throughout. Like Krebs Basin, it is a very popular camping and fishing area. From Upper Chain Lake, it is about 6 miles to Lake Atwood, though several lakes are closer.

Lake Atwood is a large glacial lake at the head of Atwood Creek at timberline. Because of the dam, the level fluctuates 16 feet during the summer. It is a popular lake and good camping places are in patches of timber on three sides. Allred Lake (34 acres) lies just south of the dam on Atwood Lake. It too has abundant camp sites. Allen Lake (Mount Emmons Lake) is another small lake sitting at the head of Atwood Creek just above Allred Lake.

Atwood Basin has fairly level, rolling terrain until you get to Lake George Beard, about 2 miles west of Lake Atwood. It lies about 1/4 mile to the southwest from where the trail starts climbing to Trail Rider Pass. About 7 acres in size, it lies in open, boggy terrain just below the pass. Two other slightly larger lakes lie just south of this one against the mountain, and drain into Lake Atwood. This area is alpine tundra with limited camping.

Trail Rider Pass

The climb to Trail Rider Pass from Atwood Basin is about 800 feet over about a mile of steep climbs and switchbacks. From the top at 11,800 feet, you descend about 500 feet into the head of Painter Basin. The trail swings across the basin about 3 miles to join the North Fork Trail just below the Highline Trail. There is a cross-country route from the base of this pass to the Highline Trail below Anderson Pass that is a direct route to Kings Peak. There is no trail, but it is open country and the route is easy to see. You just go northwest, following the upper edge of the basin.

Branch Trails from the Atwood Basin Trail

Atwood Creek

Don't try to go down this stream to reach the Uinta River Trail. The river is in a 400- to 500-foot deep gorge in this area and the trail is on the other side. You can't get across to it.

Cross-Country Route to Painter Lakes

There is an unofficial and unmaintained trail going from the north base of Roberts Pass, past Painter Lakes, and on to North Fork Park where you join the Uinta River Trail. This unmarked trail goes northeast across Atwood Creek, then swings around the end of the mountain and up Painter Draw into the Painter Lakes area on the other side of the mountain. To get to North Fork Park from here, go to Craig Lake, then northeast around the mountain-end, then up the draw north to the park.

Off-trail Routes to Lakes in Atwood Basin

Carrot Lake and B-29 Lake are smaller lakes, off the main trail a couple of miles west of Roberts Pass and above the more heavily used lakes. There is no maintained trail to any of the lakes in the basin other than Lake Atwood. These lakes have many campsites, mostly on the north, and are less visited so they should have possibilities for solitude.

B-29 Lake is 1/4 mile south of the trail against the mountain. Carrot Lake sits against the mountain about 1/2 mile west of B-29 Lake. You can reach it from the Atwood Trail by turning left (southwest) up Atwood Creek 1/2 mile, then going straight south another 1/2 mile.

Roberts Lake (23 acres) lies in a glacial cirque above Lake Atwood, at the base of the ridge northwest of Mount Emmons. It is about a mile west of Allen Lake and is best reached by following Atwood Creek up past Allen Lake. About 1/2 mile past Allen Lake, go straight west up the draw to Roberts Lake. It is in completely open tundra and is a cold, windy place for a backpacking camp.

Mount Emmons Summit (Elevation 13,440)

There are several routes from Atwood Basin to the crest of the Mount Emmons ridge. All involve off-trail hiking up moderately steep spur ridges. This is open country so landmarks can be seen all the way and you do not have to fight your way through brush or pick your way through cliffs. The climb to Mount Emmons from

Atwood Basin is easier than scrambling up boulder fields from the Timothy Lakes area. However, the approach from the trailhead is longer.

The view from on top is incredible in every direction. The ridge top is rounded and grass-covered and you can continue for a long way in either direction across minor summits.

Highline Trail - Anderson Pass to Fox Lake

The Highline Trail continues east from Anderson Pass, dropping into Painter Basin. The trail coming from Henrys Fork crosses Gunsight Pass and joins the Highline Trail about 3 miles east of Anderson Pass.

Going east, 1/2 mile brings you to another junction at Painter Basin. The Highline Trail goes left, while the right fork follows the Uinta River to connect with the main Uinta River Trail coming up from Smokey Springs. Just 1/4 mile along trail to the right is another junction with the trail that goes back west and south across Trail Rider Pass to Lake Atwood. This is a confusing area so be sure you take the correct trail.

Upper Uinta River drainage — looking south from Kings Peak.
Dave Wallace Photo

The Highline Trail stays fairly high from Painter Basin clear to Kidney Lakes, with only a gentle drop and climb as it crosses the river. About 2 more miles east on the Highline Trail, a trail takes off to the right (southeast) and goes down to North Fork Park. Continuing east on the Highline Trail you reach Kidney Lakes after another 1 1/2 miles. There are two lakes, about 100 yards apart, both about 20 acres in size. East Kidney is a little deeper and probably has the better fishing of the two. Both have many good campsites but this is a high-use area.

Just east of Kidney Lakes is the junction of the Highline Trail with the main trail up the Uinta River from U-bar Ranch. From here it is 11 miles west to Anderson Pass and 4 miles east to Fox Lake. From the Uinta River Trail junction, the Highline Trail continues east on about the same level and crosses Samuels Creek in about 2 miles. This stream comes out of Samuels Lake, about 1 1/2 miles above.

Fox Lake is a large lake (reservoir). It is in the middle of Fox Basin at the head of Shale Creek on the Highline Trail. It fluctuates 20 feet through the summer but even so is a popular lake for camping and fishing for cutthroat and brook trout.

The Highline Trail continues along the north side of Fox Lake and climbs to North Pole Pass where it leaves the Wilderness and continues east to the Chepeta Lake Trailhead. The Divide Lake Trail branches from Fox Lake and goes north 3 miles to Island Lake where it connects to trails from the Hoop Lake and Spirit Lake Trailheads. The West Fork of Whiterocks River Trail goes along the south side of Fox Lake, crosses Fox-Queant pass on the Wilderness boundary and continues down to the West Fork Trailhead.

Continuing east on the Highline Trail from Fox Lake, you climb to Brook Lake in a mile. Brook Lake is 10 acres and sits on the stream above Fox in mostly open country at the base of the mountain. It has campsites and contains both brook and cutthroat trout.

About a mile east of Brook Lake on the Highline Trail you reach North Pole Pass, on the east boundary of the Wilderness. Beyond the pass the Highline Trail enters the Whiterocks River drainage and continues east to Chepeta Lake Trailhead.

Branch Trails from the Highline Trail

Anderson Pass to Trail Rider Pass

Going from Anderson Pass to Trail Rider Pass there is a cross-country route. Skirt the base of Kings Peak, swinging to the south and east, and follow the terrain and stay high all the way to Trail Rider Pass. This saves several miles of hiking out into the basin and back again on the trails.

Gilbert Creek Trail

About 3 miles from the trail junction in Painter Basin a trail, not on the Forest Service map, cuts off to the left (north) going up Gilbert Creek and ends at the lakes in the basin below Gilbert Peak. This is an isolated area with spectacular open country but limited shelter for camping spots.

Davis-Samuel Lake Trail from Highline Trail

There are several trails in the Kidney Lakes area which are not accurately shown on the maps; however, you have little trouble getting to your destination. From Kidney Lakes, there is a trail going north called the Davis Lake-Samuel Lake Trail. It is 6 miles long, passing both Davis and Samuel Lakes and connecting again to the Highline Trail farther east.

North and South Davis Lakes lie directly north of Kidney Lakes, up the drainage about a mile. This is a pair of smaller lakes stocked with brook trout. The best campsites are on the south.

From Davis Lake the trail goes across, generally east, to near Samuels Lake, about 3 miles away. There are plenty of good campsites here and plenty of small fish in the lake. Try flies in the evening. The trail drops down south again from Samuels Lake to rejoin the Highline Trail.

Just north of Kidney Lakes, a trail branches off to the northwest and crosses over to Rainbow Lake in about a mile. This is a fairly large (35 acres), deep lake sitting above timberline in the open. Naturally reproducing brook trout are taken here. Only poor, unprotected campsites are available.

Dime Lake Trail

Branching off the Highline Trail about 3/4 mile west of Fox Lake, an unmarked trail heads north for about 1/2 mile to Dime Lake. This route requires some route finding. Two lakes sit about

1/4 mile apart on a stream connecting them. Both have been stocked with brook trout and have excellent campsites.

West Fork of Whiterocks Trail

The trail that crosses Fox-Queant Pass and descends to the West Fork of Whiterocks Trailhead branches south from the Highline Trail at Fox Lake. This is the shortest route from Fox Lake to a road.

Crescent Lake is shaped like it is named, curving around the base of a mountain. It is a reservoir so size varies. It has good campsites but is heavily used by groups. It lies just 1/4 mile south of Fox Lake on the trail .

Divide Lake Trail - Fox Lake to Island Lake

This trail goes north from Fox Lake, past Divide Lake and down to Island Lake, where one can go on out to Spirit Lake Lodge (about 9 miles) or go to Hoop Lake Campground (about the same distance). This trail is heavily used because the route to Fox Basin coming from the north is 8 or 10 miles shorter than up the Uinta River. Leaving Fox Lake and going north it's not much of a climb to the pass, as you're pretty high to start with. You go through open country and climb maybe 600 feet in about 1 1/2 miles to the ridge.

Divide Lake sits about 1/2 mile south of the ridge on the Divide Lake Trail, about 1 mile north of Fox Lake. It's about 19 acres in size, sitting in an open, windswept basin with no campsites. At 11,217 feet, this is one of the highest lakes in the Uintas. It has been stocked with cutthroat trout.

West Fork of Whiterocks Trailhead

Destination	Miles One Way	Elevation Gain
Queant Lake	3 1/2	650
Fox Pass & Wilderness Boundary	5 1/2	1400
Highline Trail at Fox Lake	7	-600 from pass

USGS Maps: Rasmussen Lakes, Chepeta Lake, Fox Lake

The new trailhead on the West Fork of Whiterocks River gives easy access to several nice lakes outside the Wilderness and is a good route to the upper end of the Uinta River Drainage.

The spur road to the West Fork of Whiterocks Trail leads west from the road to Chepeta Lake. The Forest Service has upgraded the 1 1/2 mile spur road to the West Fork Trailhead and has constructed a modern trailhead area. Follow the access road directions for Chepeta Lake Trailhead to reach the West Fork turnoff which is 25.8 miles north of the town of Whiterocks and 6.9 miles south of the end of the road at Chepeta Lake.

West Fork of Whiterocks Trail

This trail goes from the new trailhead up the West Fork of the Whiterocks River through a lake-filled basin to the head where it crosses a pass and descends to join the Highline Trail between Fox Lake and Crescent Lake. Sections of this trail have been reconstructed recently and it is a good trail for hikers and for horses. It is a short trail; you can hike in to Fox Lake from the road end in about 4 hours.

This access to Fox Lake is a more scenic route than coming up the Uinta River since you are near timberline, but the climb across the Fox-Queant Pass into Crescent Lake is a steep climb, quite a bit steeper than the North Pole Pass coming from Chepeta Lake. The trail from Chepeta Lake is at timberline almost all the way so it's prettier, but longer and slower.

Rasmussen Lakes are near the trailhead and close to the ridge to the southwest of the trail. They are reached by off-trail hiking following the outlet stream up the timbered, rocky slope. There are a few good campsites near these lakes.

Queant and Cleveland Lakes are heavily used by people hiking in about 4 miles on the West Fork Trail. These large lakes have good campsites all around. From these two lakes it is only an hour's walk over to Fox and Crescent Lakes, so people can camp in the Whiterocks drainage and day hike across the pass to fish and explore the upper Uinta River drainage. *[Duke Moscon]*

Queant Lake Primitive Road

A primitive road starts 1.3 miles north of the spur road to the West Fork Trailhead and heads west along the north side of the West Fork of the Whiterocks River. This road is currently open to vehicles but it is lightly used and requires a high-clearance vehicle or 4WD. It provides an alternative access to the Queant Lake area.

Bear Safety in Backpacker Country

There are a lot of people in Utah, even in the Wilderness, and not very many bears. Bears generally avoid humans but humans enjoy walking though bear country. Bear safety is important.

If hikers and campers behave in ways that invite the bears to scrounge for food in human camps the outcome will always be bad for the bear. In a human - bear encounter the bear is the endangered party. It usually ends up dead.

Sometimes the bear is killed by a frightened person shooting "in defense of life or property," or it becomes a target for the professional game control officers.

Everyone who believes that the Wilderness is the home of wild critters needs to help protect bears by following a few simple rules.

• Never attempt to feed a bear or approach it to take pictures.

• Do not leave garbage, food scraps, or fish guts on the ground.

• If you see a bear at close range, make noise, yell, or bang pots to scare it away. Keep calm and retreat slowly until the bear leaves.

Chepeta Lake Trailhead

Destination	Miles One Way	Elevation Gain
Reader Lakes	3	400
North Pole Pass & Wilderness Boundary	6 1/2	1900
Fox Lake	8 1/2	-1400 from pass

USGS Maps: Chepeta Lake, Fox Lake

Chepeta Lake is at 10,600 feet making this one of the highest trailheads in the Uintas. Timberline is only a few minutes' walk from the car and you are surrounded by the open ridges typical of the Uintas high country.

To get the Chepeta Lake area, take Utah 121 north and east from Roosevelt for 15 miles or west from Vernal for 24 miles to a junction where Utah 121 makes a right-angle turn. Coming from Vernal on 121, the road to Whiterocks is straight ahead. Coming from Roosevelt through Neola, the road to Whiterocks is a left turn. Continue north through the town of Whiterocks and note your mileage as you pass the Whiterocks Post Office. The paved road to Uinta Canyon is on the left 3.6 miles north of the Post Office, and the road to Chepeta Lakes is straight ahead.

The pavement narrows at a junction 6.9 miles from Whiterocks where the road to Chepeta Lake is again straight ahead and the road to the right leads to lower Whiterocks Canyon. A mile farther is the Forest Service Elkhorn Guard Station. Here the pavement ends and you make a left turn onto a gravel road marked "Elkhorn Loop," cross a cattle guard and go past the Ashley National Forest boundary sign.

The road begins climbing from sagebrush country into aspen and then into lodgepole pine as it ascends. There are many side roads, many going to timber sale areas, but the main road is well maintained and easy to distinguish. The Elkhorn Loop road turns west at a junction 22.1 miles from Whiterocks. The loop goes past Pole Creek Lake and on to Uinta Canyon and is a rough but passable gravel road. The route to Chepeta Lake continues north as a graded road. The spur road to the West Fork of Whiterocks Trailhead turns left 25.8 miles from Whiterocks and the Chepeta Lake road continues straight.

The trailhead parking for passenger cars is a graded area on the side of the road 32.8 miles from Whiterocks. Beyond here the road becomes 4WD as it fords the stream coming from Chepeta Lake then climbs up the other side and continues for a final 0.4 mile to the Chepeta Lake dam. There are no campgrounds near here but there are areas along the road where you can car camp.

Several trails can be reached from Chepeta Lake. The Highline Trail touches a road here for the first time since leaving the Mirror Lake Highway. The Highline Trail west to the Wilderness boundary is heavily used and can be easily followed, but the continuation east is not regularly maintained and may be hard to follow.

Highline Trail - West to Fox Lake

The westbound Highline Trail goes across the dam, passes a signboard, and enters the trees. This is a well-used trail with a distinct tread and is marked with blazes. From Chepeta Lake you can enter the Wilderness Area by taking the Highline Trail to North Pole Pass, above the Fox Lake Basin. This trail to Fox Lake is at or above timberline almost all the way, so it's a more scenic access than from the West Fork Trailhead, but it's a little longer trail.

Reader Lake is a shallow pond along the trail and has campsites nearby. Taylor Lake is 2 miles farther and is a deep lake with a rocky shore and few campsites. A connecting trail leads south from Taylor Lake to join the West Fork Trail at Queant Lake.

Beyond Taylor Lake the trail goes northwest staying high on an open ridge and climbs to North Pole Pass overlooking Fox Lake. The eastern boundary of the Wilderness is at the pass and runs south along the ridge from there. The open ridge offers opportunities for off-trail hiking. One possibility is to hike to the Uinta crest and look down on the lakes in the Burnt Fork drainage.

Highline Trail - East to Leidy Peak

The eastbound Highline Trail can be found where the road fords the stream below the lake. Going east, the Highline Trail crosses the head of the Whiterocks River drainage, enters Lakeshore Basin, and traverses under Leidy Peak. The area between Chepeta Lakes and Leidy Peak was proposed for wilderness designation in 1984, and although it lacks official protection it remains a natural and roadless area with significant wilderness values. The trails in this area are neither well maintained nor heavily used. The Highline Trail meets a road again at the Leidy Peak Trailhead.

Upper Basin Trail

Moccasin, Papoose and Wigwam Lakes are all within 1/2 mile to the northeast of Chepeta Lake. The trail starts as a road scar at the east end of the dam and is well marked. Beyond Moccasin Lake the trail branches to form a loop connecting Wigwam and Papoose Lakes. These lakes are right at timberline and outstanding off-trail hiking opportunities exist on the ridges above. One possibility is to continue up the drainage past Wigwam Lake to the saddle overlooking the Spirit Lake area. The area is rocky but there are some good campsites. *[Reni Stott]*

Reader Lakes Trail

Signs and maps show a trail going from the road to Reader Lakes. This route follows the stream and you won't get lost, but parts of the trail are difficult to find on the ground.

Moccasin Lake near Chepeta Lake Trailhead
John Veranth Photo

Leidy Peak Trailhead

Destination	Miles One Way	Elevation Gain
Leidy Peak Summit	1 1/2	1000
Upper Lakeshore Basin	5 1/2	200
Pass to Whiterocks Drainage	7 1/2	400 net gain
Chepeta Lake	21 1/2	-1000 from pass

USGS Maps: Leidy Peak, Whiterocks Lake, Chepeta Lake

The High Bollies at the far east end of the High Uintas is a little known and largely unprotected area that has the same high-quality wilderness values that are found in the designated area to the west. A reintroduced herd of bighorn sheep is occasionally seen here. This area was not included in the 1984 legislation but wilderness advocates continue to work for protection of this area. Someday this roadless area may be designated as Wilderness or altered by timber cutting. The area is currently managed as multiple use forest and represents another precious remnant of the ever shrinking roadless lands. It is certainly worth visiting now.

This area is not as heavily used as the areas to the east and the Vernal District of the Ashley Forest does not regularly maintain the backcountry trails so route finding will be part of your experience. That is no problem since the trailhead is almost at timberline and landmarks are visible everywhere. Use common sense and a topographic map to follow your route.

The road access to this area is a 9-mile spur road to Hacking Lake that branches from the Red Cloud Loop road north of Vernal. The Red Cloud Loop is managed as a scenic drive and is well maintained and marked by Forest Service signs. One end of the Red Cloud Loop starts on US 191 at a marked junction 19.9 miles north of US 40 in Vernal. Follow the paved road for 3.3 miles to a turnoff on a gravel road. Follow the Red Cloud Loop signs for 12.1 miles to the Hacking Lake turnoff.

Another route from Vernal is to take the Red Cloud Loop in the opposite direction starting from Utah 121 at 3500 West on the Vernal street grid. Follow the paved road for 13 miles past the Dry Fork Cemetery and into the mouth of a narrow canyon. The road passes a junction for Brownie Canyon 2.5 miles from the end of the pavement, then begins to climb switchbacks onto the plateau and continues past the Y-junction for Ashley Twin Lakes. The turnoff to Hacking Lake is a T-junction 34.1 miles from Utah 121.

The spur road from the Red Cloud Loop to the trailhead is 9.1 miles long. Go straight at each junction; do not take any of the turnoffs to the right until you reach the road to Hacking Lake in 8 miles. Here the road to the trailhead goes right and climbs a final mile to a turnaround where there is room to park. The last 4 miles are somewhat rough but suitable for passenger cars.

Highline Trail - West to Chepeta Lake(#025)

The trail starts from the turnaround at the road closure gate. Leidy Peak is visible straight ahead. The Highline Trail goes southwest from here and traverses below Leidy Peak staying above timberline. There are trails on both the north and south sides of Leidy Peak. A branch trail drops from the Highline Trail into Lakeshore Basin and connects with the road to Ashley Twin Lakes. The trail between here and Chepeta Lake is lightly used and it is difficult to follow since there is often no distinct track. Be sure to follow the landmarks using your map. There are some cairns marking the route above timberline.

This is a high-elevation trail. It stays between 10,500 and 11,500 feet along the south side of the divide all the way to Chepeta Lake. After passing several cirque lakes at the upper edge of the Lakeshore Basin the trail climbs over Gabbro Pass and drops down to Deadman Lake at the head of Dry Fork. Deadman Lake is in open terrain but has some campsites to the south. It is at the end of a trail coming up Dry Fork. The Highline Trail then crosses into the Whiterocks drainage and passes Whiterocks Lake, an active reservoir. The trail then gets farther from the main ridge as it heads toward the stream coming from Chepeta Lake.

Leidy Peak Summit (Elevation 12,028)

The crest of the Uinta Mountains is gentle and rounded in this area and lacks the cliffs and cirque walls that make off-trail route finding more difficult farther west. From the Leidy Peak Trailhead the route up Leidy Peak is an off-trail hike ascending any one of the grass-covered spur ridges to the top.

Bibliography

Fishing

Division of Wildlife Resources Staff: *Lakes of the High Uintas* . A 10 volume series with each volume covering two or three drainages. For each lake the books describe the acreage and depth, the fish species present, and sometimes the camping and horse pasture conditions (as of the mid-1980's). The inexpensive books are available from DWR offices.

Wixom, Hartt: *Fishing and Hunting Guide to Utah*, Wasatch Publishers, Salt Lake City, 1990. A guidebook to the state by a long-time outdoor writer.

Human and Natural History

Bryant, Bruce: Geologic and Structure Maps of the Salt Lake City 1° x 2° Quadrangle. U.S. Geological Survey, 1992. A spectacularly detailed full-color geologic map covering the High Uintas west of Kings Peak.

Fradkin, Philip L.: *Sagebrush Country - Land and the American West,* Alfred A. Knopf Co., New York, 1989. An enjoyable account alternating a travelog of the author's hike along the Highline Trail with the history of settlement and development along both the North and South Slopes of the Uintas. It has an extensive bibliography for those who want to read more.

Hansen, Wallace R.: *The Geologic Story of the Uinta Mountains*, U.S. Geological Survey Bulletin 1291, 1975. A good semi-technical introduction with bibliography. Available from USGS offices.

Hayward, Lynn C.: *The High Uintas - Utah's Land of Lakes and Forest*, Monte L. Bean Life Science Museum, Provo, Utah, 1983. Flora, fauna, geology, and the history of early explorations.

Address List

Wasatch National Forest

Supervisors Office
8226 Federal Building
125 South State Street
Salt Lake City, 84111
Phone (801) 524-5030

Naturalist Basin Area
Kamas Ranger District
50 East Center Street
P.O Box 68
Kamas, Utah 84036
(801) 783-4338

Bear River & Blacks Fork Drainage
Evanston Ranger District
P.O. Box 1880
Evanston, Wyoming 82930
(307) 789-3194

Smiths Fork, Henrys Fork, and Hoop Lake
Mountain View Ranger District
Lone Tree Road, Highway 44
Mountain View, Wyoming 82939
(307) 782-6555

Citizen Groups

Wilderness & Wildlife Protection
Utah Wilderness Association
455 East 400 South #306
Salt Lake City, Utah 84111
(801) 359-1337

Outdoor Activities
Wasatch Mountain Club
888 South 200 East #207
Salt Lake City, Utah 84111

Activities & Advocacy
Sierra Club, Utah Chapter
177 East 900 South
Salt Lake City, Utah 84111

Ashley National Forest

Supervisors Office
353 N. Vernal Ave
Vernal, Utah 84078
(801) 789-1181

Grandaddy Basin & Rock Creek
Duchesne Ranger District
85 West Main, P.O. Box 1
Duchesne, Utah 84021
(801) 738-2482

Lake Fork to Uinta River Drainage
Roosevelt Ranger District
West Highway 40, P.O. Box 338
Roosevelt, Utah 84066
(801) 722-5018

Whiterocks to Leidy Peak
Vernal Ranger District
353 N. Vernal Ave
Vernal, Utah 84078
(801) 789-1181

Spirit Lake
Flaming Gorge Ranger District
P.O. Box 278
Manila, Utah 84046
(801) 784-3445

Utah Division of Wildlife Resources

North Slope of Uintas
Northern Region
515 East 5300 South
Ogden, Utah 84405-4599
(801) 479-5143

South Slope of Uintas
Northeast Region
153 East 100 North
Vernal, Utah 84078
(801) 789-3103

Index

Authors

John Veranth began hiking and rock climbing in New England and first visited the Uintas in 1972. Two years later he moved to Utah to be close to the mountains. He works as an engineer and is an environmental activist concentrating on trailhead access and wilderness protection issues. He serves on the boards of the Utah Wilderness Association and of the Wasatch Mountain Club. Previous books are *Hiking the Wasatch* and *Wasatch Winter Trails*.

Mel Davis grew up in Idaho, began hiking and backpacking there, and has been hiking Utah's mountains for nearly 30 years. He worked as a news writer and photographer and as the regional photographer for the Bureau of Reclamation. In the early 1970s he helped write the original *Wasatch Trails*. He started Wasatch Publishers, and continued writing and publishing outdoor books. He is now retired and is traveling and enjoying his grandchildren and great-grandchildren.

Other Wasatch Publishers Books

Wind River Trails by Finis Mitchell. Wasatch Publishers, 1975 (8th Printing 1991). A hiking and fishing guide to Wyoming's Wind River Range by the man who first stocked these mountain lakes with fish by horseback and who has been hiking in the Wind River Range since the 1930s.

Hiking The Wasatch by John Veranth. Wasatch Mountain Club c/o Wasatch Publishers, 1988 (revised 1991). A hiking and natural history guide to the trails from City Creek Canyon to American Fork Canyon.

Park City Trails by Raye Ringholz. Wasatch Publishers, 1984. Covers hikes and ski tours that are readily accessible from Park City, Utah.

Wasatch Winter Trails by John Veranth. Wasatch Publishers, 1991. A ski touring and snowshoe guidebook for the central Wasatch and the western Uintas near Kamas.

Cache Tours by Ann Schimpf and Scott Datwyler. Wasatch Publishers, 1977. A ski touring guide to the mountains around Logan, Utah.

Wasatch Quartzite by John Gottman, foreword by Harold Goodrow. Wasatch Mountain Club c/o Wasatch Publishers, 1979. A rock climbing guide to many moderate climbs and scrambles near Big Cottonwood Canyon. Includes a history of the early days of climbing in the Wasatch.

Fishing and Hunting Guide to Utah by Hartt Wixom. Wasatch Publishers, 1990. If you are new to the state or just looking for new places to fish, this book can be your guide. The author is a long-time outdoor writer and environmentalist who shares his knowledge of the lakes, streams, and reservoirs of Utah.

These books are available in local bookstores and outdoor shops and are available by mail order from the publisher. Send for a complete list of titles and prices.

Wasatch Publishers
4460 Ashford Drive
Salt Lake City, Utah 84124